D0874220

TWAYNE'S WORLD AUTHORS SERIES

A Survey of the World's Literature

Luis Davila, Indiana University

EDITOR

José Donoso

TWAS 517

José Donoso

JOSÉ DONOSO

By GEORGE R. McMURRAY
Colorado State University

TWAYNE PUBLISHERS
A DIVISION OF G. K. HALL & CO., BOSTON

Published in 1979 by Twayne Publishers,
A Division of G. K. Hall & Co.
All Rights Reserved

Printed on permanent/durable acid-free paper and bound
in the United States of America

First Printing

(Street)
PQ8097
.D617Z77

Library of Congress Cataloging in Publication Data

McMurray, George R., 1925–
José Donoso.

(Twayne's world authors series ; TWAS 517 : Chile)
Bibliography: p. 171–74
Includes index.
1. Donoso, José, 1924–   —Criticism and interpretation.
PQ8097.D617Z77   863   78-15574
ISBN 0-8057-6358-9

To my wife

Contents

About the Author

Preface

Chronology

1. The Man and His Times   15

2. The Short Stories   34

3. A Period of Transition (1957–1966)   59

4. Myth and the Absurd: *Hell Has No Limits*   89

5. *The Obscene Bird of Night:* A Tribute to Consciousness   108

6. *Sacred Families:* Middle-Class Reality and Fantasy   138

7. Concluding Remarks   148

Notes and References   153

Selected Bibliography   171

Index   175

About the Author

George R. McMurray is a native of Grinnell, Iowa and holds the Ph.D. in Romance Languages from the University of Nebraska. He is presently Professor of Spanish and Latin American Literature at Colorado State University, Fort Collins, Colorado. He is the author of *Gabriel García Márquez* and has published articles and reviews on contemporary Latin-American fiction in various journals including *Hispania*, *World Literature Today*, *Nueva Narrativa Hispanoamericana*, *Revista de la Universidad de México*, *Modern Language Quarterly*, *Chasqui*, and *Saturday Review*. Professor McMurray is currently working on a monograph on the Argentine writer, Jorge Luis Borges.

Preface

Since Pablo Neruda's death in 1973 José Donoso is probably the most widely known living Chilean writer both at home and abroad. That he has achieved an audience outside Chile is demonstrated by the numerous translations of his novels, all of which have appeared in several of the major western languages. The present study is the first book-length treatment of Donoso's fiction to be published in English, its purpose being to serve the general reading public as a guide to a better understanding of his life and works.

José Donoso (1924) has published seventeen short stories, four novels, three novelettes, and an autobiographical account of his role in present-day Spanish-American letters. In addition, he has penned many journalistic articles, critical essays, and translations that have not been discussed in this study. Three of the short stories have been dealt with in footnotes because of their minor importance. The works are treated in chronological order with the exception of the short stories, which are analyzed in Chapter II, and *Historia personal del "boom," (The Boom in Spanish American Literature A Personal History)* which is discussed in Chapter I under the heading "Donoso and the 'Boom.' " *Coronación (Coronation)* and *Este domingo (This Sunday)* have been incorporated into Chapter III because together they indicate a transitional phase in the author's total literary production. Separate chapters have been devoted to *El lugar sin límites (Hell Has No Limits)*, *El obsceno pájaro del la noche* (The Obscene Bird of Night) and *Tres novelitas burguesas (Sacred Families)*.

Special attention has been given to the technical procedures and thematic content of Donoso's works which owe their universality to his aesthetic sensitivity and keen insights into human nature. Because his writings are still relatively recent, critical material on them is somewhat limited. For this reason, the majority of the judgments made here are mine. The discussions of existentialist philosophy are based primarily on Jean-Paul Sartre's theories of atheistic existentialism.

Generally speaking, titles have been rendered in both Spanish and English the first time they are mentioned. Thereafter only the

English title is used if the work has appeared in English, and only the Spanish, if it has not been translated. The quotations from the four novels and "Paseo" are taken from the English translations of these works. All other English translations are my own.

For the privilege of interviewing Mr. Donoso in his home in Spain I am deeply grateful to both him and his wife. I should also like to express my thanks to Mr. Donoso's father, Dr. José Donoso, for allowing me to visit him and Mrs. Donoso, now deceased, in Santiago, Chile. Acknowledgement is made to the following companies for their permission to quote passages from Mr. Donoso's works: E. P. Dutton & Co., Inc.; Alfred A. Knopf, Inc.; Editorial Seix Barral, S. A.; Editorial Anagrama; Brandt & Brandt (New York); and Agencia Literaria Carmen Balcells (Barcelona). Finally, a word of appreciation is due to Colorado State University for its generous support of this study.

Chronology

1924   October 5: José Donoso born in Santiago, Chile, first child of Dr. José Donoso and Alicia Yáñez.

1932–   Studied at an English school, "The Grange."
1942

1943   Dropped out of school.

1945–   Worked on the pampas as a sheepherder in Magallanes, the
1946   southern tip of Chile.

1946–   Hitchhiked through Patagonia to Buenos Aires where he
1947   worked as a dockhand.

1947   Returned to Chile, finished high school and enrolled in the University of Chile, specializing in English.

1949–   Studied English literature at Princeton University with the
1951   aid of a Doherty Foundation Scholarship. Published his first two stories, "The Blue Woman" and "The Poisoned Pastries," in *MSS*, a Princeton literary review.

1951   Awarded the B.A. degree. Traveled through Mexico and Central America.

1952   Returned to Chile and began to teach English at the Kent School and at the Pedagogical Institute of the Catholic University in Santiago.

1954   Published "China" (China), his first short story written in Spanish.

1955   Published *Veraneo y otros cuentos* (Summertime and Other Stories) which won the Santiago Municipal Short Story Prize.

1956   Published *Dos cuentos* (Two Stories).

1957   Published *Coronación (Coronation)*, his first novel.

1958–   Spent two years in Buenos Aires.
1960

1959   Published "Pasos en la noche" (Footsteps in the Night), "La puerta cerrada" (The Closed Door), and "Paseo" (Walk).

1960   Returned to Chile and became a reporter for the weekly news magazine *Ercilla*. Published "El charleston" (Charleston), a collection of stories containing "El charleston" and four other stories published previously.

1961   Married María del Pilar Serrano, a Chilean painter he had met in Buenos Aires.

1962   Published "Santelices" (Santelices). Began to lecture in the College of Journalism at the University of Chile. Became editor of *Ercilla* and the magazine's leading literary critic.

1963   *Coronation* won the Faulkner Foundation Prize for the best postwar Chilean novel.

1964   "El hombrecito" ("The 'Hombrecito' ") published in English. Attended Writers' Congress at Chichén Itzá, Mexico.

1965   *Coronation* published in English. Published Los mejores cuentos de José Donoso (The Best Stories of José Donoso). This book contains his fourteen most important stories, all of which had appeared previously.

1965–
1967   Lectured in the Writers' Workshop at the University of Iowa.

1966   Published *Este domingo (This Sunday)* and *El lugar sin límites (Hell Has No Limits)*.

1967   *This Sunday* and "Ana María" published in English. The Donosos moved to Mallorca and adopted an infant daughter.

1968   Received his first Guggenheim Award.

1969   Was guest editor for two numbers of *TriQuarterly* devoted to contemporary Latin American letters. "Paseo" published in English under Spanish title. Lectured briefly at Colorado State University where illness forced him to undergo surgery for a bleeding ulcer. Moved to Barcelona.

1970   Published *El obsceno pájaro de la noche (The Obscene Bird of Night)*.

1971   Moved to Calaceite, Teruel, southwest of Barcelona. *Cuentos* (Stories) published, containing the fourteen stories included in *Los mejores cuentos de José Donoso*.

1972   Published *Historia personal del "boom" (The Boom in Spanish American Literature A Personal History)*. Hell Has No Limits published in English in a volume entitled *Triple Cross*, with two other short Latin American novels.

1973   Published *Tres novelitas burguesas (Sacred Families)*. The Obscene Bird of Night published in English. Received his second Guggenheim Award.

1975   Lectured at Princeton University. Returned to Chile for a short visit.

Chronology

1976   Moved with his family to Sitges, near Barcelona.
1977   Published in English *The Boom in Spanish American Literature A Personal History, Charleston & Other Stories,* and *Sacred Families.* Mr. Donoso is working on a novel to be entitled *Casa de campo* (Country House).

CHAPTER 1

The Man and His Times

I *Literary Backgrounds*

JOSÉ Donoso is not only Chile's most widely known living writer of prose fiction but, according to critic Cedomil Goic in his book on the Chilean novel, "the most outstanding and prestigious figure of the present generation."[1] Perhaps a better understanding of his works, which are viewed with increasing interest and appreciation abroad, can be achieved if they are considered within the broad framework of twentieth century Chilean and Latin American letters.

The most important single movement in the Spanish American novel during the first half of the present century was a literary school known as Regionalism or, as it is frequently called in Chile, *Criollismo*. (Applied to people, the term *criollo* formerly signified a descendent of European colonists, but eventually it was used to refer to anybody born in Spanish America. In reference to things, *criollo* has come to be almost synonymous with native or American as opposed to foreign.[2]) *Criollismo*, then, is basically a realistic literary movement which conveys a strong flavor of Spanish-American life, with special emphasis on rural landscapes and provincial customs. This type of fiction, whose roots go back to nineteenth century Spain's *Costumbrismo* and *Realismo*,[3] incorporated positivistic aspects of French Naturalism as well as some elements of Modernism, a school that emphasized aesthetic essence and sought to renovate Spanish American literature between 1885 and 1915. Generally speaking, *Criollismo* utilized traditional novelistic techniques and a photographic style, often colored with local speech patterns, to depict man's vain struggles against an overpowering natural or social environment. As the term Regionalism suggests, these works frequently focused on issues related to a given locality or country rather than on universal themes or values.

Outstanding Regionalist novels include such well-known titles as
Mariano Azuela's *Los de abajo (The Underdogs)*, 1915, which depicts episodes of the Mexican Revolution; *La vorágine (The Vortex)*,
1924, by José Eustasio Rivera, a tragic story of love, exploitation,
and violence set in the Colombian jungles; *Don Segundo Sombra
(Don Segundo Sombra)*, 1926, Ricardo Güiraldes' poetic portrayal of
cowboy life on the Argentine pampas; *Doña Bárbara (Doña Bárbara)*, 1929, by Rómulo Gallegos, a symbolic dramatization of the
struggle between civilization and barbarism on the Venezuelan
plains; Jorge Icaza's *Huasipungo (The Villagers)*, 1934, which describes the wretched existence of the Ecuadorian Indian; and *El
mundo es ancho y ajeno (Broad and Alien is the World)*, 1941, by
Ciro Alegría, a beautifully written Peruvian novel about the futile
efforts of Indians to keep possession of their land and preserve their
communal way of life.

Chilean *Criollistas* include Mariano Latorre, leader of his nation's
Regionalist school, Baldomero Lillo, Luis Durand, Marta Brunet,
José Santos González Vera, and Eduardo Barrios.[4] Two of the finest
examples of Chilean Regionalist fiction are Barrios' *Gran señor y
rajadiablos* (Great Lord and Hellion), 1948, which depicts several
stages in the life of a virile, self-reliant landowner representing a
reactionary remnant of the nation's feudal oligarchy, and Durand's
Frontera (Frontier), 1949, a prose epic of love and violence portraying the taming of southern Chile's wilderness in the late
nineteenth century.

During the 1930's young Chilean intellectuals became dissatisfied
with *Criollismo* which they felt no longer reflected the realities of a
country undergoing fundamental social changes wrought by immi-
gration, industrialization, and urbanization. One group of left-wing
writers who had come together at the Pedagogical Institute of the
University of Chile took advantage of the political ferment of
1938—when Pedro Aguirre Cerda was elected president by the
liberal Popular Front Party—to proclaim their opposition to the
Regionalists' outmoded methods and advocate a new type of fiction,
often referred to as neorealism. The generation of 1938 shifted the
literary focus from the country to the city and, inspired by Marx and
Lenin, strove to achieve social and political reforms by portraying
the miserable lot of the downtrodden masses. The leader of this
school was Juan Godoy whose novel *Angurrientos* (The Insatiable
Ones), 1940, describes the futile attempts of a young, idealistic

leftist to instill social consciousness in his countrymen and improve the existence of the *roto*, i.e., the poverty-stricken Chilean laborer. (The term *angurrientismo* signifies the voracious appetite for life which, according to Godoy, explains the nature of the *roto* as well as that of the common man in Chile.) Other important members of the generation of 1938 include: Nicomedes Guzmán who, like Godoy, concentrates on portraits of the proletariat; Carlos Droguett, whose works such as *Eloy* (Eloy), 1960, and *Patas de perro* (Dog's Feet), 1965, make him the most important writer of the group; and Daniel Belmar, Volodia Teitelboim, Luis Merino Reyes, Reinaldo Lomboy, Francisco Coloane, Guillermo Atías, and Fernando Alegría.

Another strong tendency in twentieth-century Chilean letters attempts to transcend the narrow limits of *Criollismo* by placing greater emphasis on imagination, psychology, universal themes, and innovative techniques. Several major authors of the older generation including Pedro Prado (1886–1952), Augusto d'Halmar (1882–1950), and Joaquín Edwards Bello (1886–1968) sought to achieve a literary synthesis of national and universal values but it was not until the mid 1930's—approximately the same time as the appearance of the generation of 1938—that a group of young, avant-garde literati, reacting against what they considered the Regionalists' superficial, picturesque portraits of rural life, initiated reforms, the repercussions of which are still felt today in Chilean fiction. These writers, the most important of whom are Benjamín Subercaseaux, Vicente Huidobro, Juan Marín, Carlos Sepúlveda Leyton, Manuel Rojas, and María Luisa Bombal, reversed the naturalistic concept of man as a static type struggling against a hostile environment and utilized modern philosophy, psychology, and literary styles to unveil the dark, irrational side of human nature. Their principal sources of inspiration included a wide variety of foreign authors such as Dostoevski, Dos Passos, Faulkner, Hemingway, Kafka, Joyce, Virginia Woolf, D. H. Lawrence, Proust, Gide, Freud, Henry Bergson, and Kierkegaard.

Two novels illustrative of the concepts of this group are highly significant for their universalizing influence on Chilean letters and their foreshadowing of future trends: *La última niebla (House of Mist)*, by María Luisa Bombal (1910), and *Hijo de ladrón* (Son of a Thief), by Manuel Rojas (1896–1973). Bombal's poetic work, first published in 1935, explores the subconscious of a young woman whose husband's indifference obliges her to seek true love and passion in her dreams. The mist pervading the protagonist's subjective world of imagination creates a hostile atmosphere of uncertainty, not unlike a surrealistic nightmare, which reduces reality to subliminal obsessions. The novel also spotlights the lack of communication and rigidity of upper-class citizens whose daily lives are dominated by superficial social conventions and whose inability to commit themselves to meaningful or creative action is expressed by the woman's final thoughts regarding her bleak future, "I'll follow him to carry out a multitude of small tasks; to perform a multitude of pleasant frivolous duties; to weep according to custom and smile out of duty. I'll follow him in order to live correctly and, some day, to die correctly."[5]

Although the reaction against *Criollismo* was well under way by the end of the 1930's, Chilean critic Fernando Alegría believes the death blow to this "stereotyped regionalism" was dealt by *Hijo de ladrón* (1951), which "marks the end of Chilean regionalism and initiates the process of criticism and self-criticism on a social level that, like an umbilical cord, connects . . . the eight or ten most significant novels of the 1960's."[6] Written in the form of a picaresque novel, this masterpiece relates the first seventeen years in the life of its protagonist who, after being abandoned as a child, wanders through parts of South America, eventually landing in prison. The book's success derives from the psychological depth of its characters, its themes of identity search and existential solitude and, perhaps even more notable, its skillful experimentation with a wide variety of new styles and techniques. Thus, through the manipulation of the narrative distance (the narrator-protagonist alternates between present and past episodes of his life) and the utilization of symbolic images representing hunger, alienation, and anguish, *Hijo de ladrón* breaks with the stylistic simplicity and chronologically ordered events of traditional realism, uncovers a multifaceted, ambiguous reality, and thrusts the reader into a universal sphere of frustration and despair.

The first allusion to the generation of 1950, of which Donoso is a representative, was made in 1956 by novelist Enrique Lafourcade in a speech on contemporary Chilean fiction delivered in Santiago.[7] Lafourcade admits that he chose the year 1950 as a label for the young group of writers principally because midcentury seemed to be a convenient temporal point of reference for his discussion. Although at first there was considerable disagreement over the existence of a genuine literary generation, Lafourcade's designation is now generally accepted by critics of contemporary Chilean letters.

The generation of 1950 became the focus of a heated controversy when, in 1959, critic Jorge Hubner attacked several of its members, including Donoso and Lafourcade, for their excessive emphasis on sordid detail and existential despair. According to Hubner, the French existentialist "philosophy of disaster" was understandable as a product of devastated postwar Europe, but hardly applicable to Chile, a nation vibrating with health and vitality.[8] Hubner's statements are misleading in some respects, but they do suggest some of the major differences between the generations of 1938 and 1950. Whereas the former was basically optimistic, with its passionate commitment to political liberty, social justice, and ethical values, members of the younger generation remained skeptically aloof from the political and social arenas and turned inward in search of their own individual philosophical and aesthetic values. Through their alienated protagonists they expressed their twentieth-century anguish over the absurdity of finite man's search for absolutes in an infinite universe and, occasionally, their ineffectual rebellion without any discernible cause. According to the critic Fernando Alegría, the common denominators of this generation are a tendency toward morbidity and an inability to take definitive action either individually or collectively.[9]

Another distinction between the two generations concerns their social backgrounds, the older group having risen principally from the lower-middle class and the younger from intellectual or wealthy upper-class families. In keeping with its pessimistic outlook on life, the generation of 1950 has repeatedly treated the physical, economic, and moral decay afflicting the Chilean oligarchy and, by implication, the world in general. Examples of novels featuring this theme include Donoso's *Coronación (Coronation)*, 1957, Margarita Aguirre's *El huésped* (The Guest), 1958, and Jorge Edward's *El peso de la noche* (The Weight of Night), 1964. Unlike the generation of 1938, which idealistically sought to improve the miserable lives of the proletariat, the more recent generation tends to portray the poor as criminal or sexual elements threatening the stability of the bourgeois establishment.[10]

Because of its reaction against the hackneyed forms of conventional realism and its ardent desire to create new literary modes, the generation of 1950 has been called *irrealista*.[11] Its multifaceted,

fragmented allusions to reality contrast with the preceding generation's attempts at total analyses and reflect an uncertain, tormented
outlook on the human condition. This pessimism is illustrated by
novels such as Lafourcade's *Pena de muerte* (Penalty of Death),
1952, which depicts the disintegration of a frustrated, homosexual
artist, and Jaime Lazo's *El cepo* (The Snare), 1958, the portrait of an
office worker trapped in a stifling routine.

Influences on the generation of 1950 include Faulkner, Woolf,
and Joyce (for their experiments in literary technique); Sartre and
Camus (for their fictional treatment of existentialism); and, begin-
ning in the late 1950's, major contemporary Latin American writers
such as Jorge Luis Borges, Ernesto Sábato, Alejo Carpentier, Juan
Carlos Onetti, Miguel Angel Asturias, and Eduardo Mallea (for their
thematic and stylistic innovations). Besides Donoso and Enrique
Lafourcade, the principal members of the group are Jaime Lazo,
Jorge Edwards, Margarita Aguirre, José Manuel Vergara, Armando
Cassígoli, Guillermo Blanco, Yerko Moretic, María E. Gertner,
Claudio Giaconi, Herbert Muller, Alfonso Echeverría, and Luís A.
Heiremans. These writers have added new dimensions to Chilean
fiction by projecting their aesthetic and philosophic preoccupations
beyond the sphere of national boundaries. This study will attempt to
demonstrate how their generation's leading representative, José
Donoso, has achieved universal stature through his writings.

II *Biography*

One of José Donoso's most salient traits is his strong sense of
individualism which has led him to abhor stereotypes and facile
categories. He admits to being highly emotional, makes no claims to
thinking or behaving in a consistently rational manner, and most
certainly would find the search for absolute values in the present-
day world of uncertainty a waste of time. Perhaps for this reason he
has refused to be very outspoken about his political convictions,
although his sympathies are unquestionably with left-wing causes.[12]
Like many writers, Donoso has injected numerous autobiographical
elements into his fictional world, thus making a knowledge of his life
an important factor in understanding his works. He was born on
October 5, 1924 in Santiago, Chile into an upper-middle-class family, the eldest of three sons. His father, for whom he was named, is a
retired medical doctor of Spanish descent and his mother, Alicia
Yáñez, was the daughter of a prominent Chilean family of Spanish

and Italian blood. The elderly couple and their servant Teresa Vergara,[13] who raised their three boys, lived in the spacious home where the author was born until the death of Mrs. Donoso in 1976. According to Donoso, his father was more interested in horse racing and cards than in his profession, "with the result that visible means of support were slender."[14] In 1929 the family moved to an immense, labyrinthian mansion belonging to Dr. Donoso's three elderly great aunts so that he could look after them as a kind of doctor in residence. The atmosphere of decrepitude and decay in this house, where José spent nine years of his childhood, was to become an obsessive theme in the future writer's fiction.

When Donoso was seven years old, his father hired an English governess, Miss Merrington, to teach his sons English, but, tiring of her rambunctious charges, she left for the northern port of Antofagasta to teach English to a little girl named María del Pilar Serrano who, by coincidence, would become José's wife many years later. Donoso's excellent knowledge of English is also due to the fact that for ten years, from 1932 until 1942, he studied at an English school in Santiago called The Grange. His ironic remarks regarding this institution give insight into his independent nature: "Right from the start I hated school, especially the compulsory sports with the alien, unreasonable standards of playing fair, keeping a stiff upper lip and being a good loser. My early rejection of this first 'collective experience' may have determined my lifelong incapacity to belong to groups of any kind—political, social or recreational."[15] Donoso's criticism of The Grange notwithstanding, his deep respect for English culture probably stems at least in part from this period of his life.

Meanwhile José's father hired a boxing instructor to make his two older sons proficient in that sport but, as might be expected, José disliked boxing just as much as he did school. "I assume that I learned how to box, but can't be sure since after my experience in the ring at home I have always been careful to stay out of scraps. . . . Boxing with my younger brother, who was taller and stronger than I, and being beaten up twice a week, I began to hate home too."[16] Because of his distaste for both school and sports, Donoso began feigning stomach-aches in order to be allowed to remain at home in bed, but much to his chagrin an appendectomy was prescribed and performed. Several years later his fake stomach pains would become a real case of gastritis, eventually leading to an ulcer.[17]

Donoso never took his religious education seriously, partly because his father was a non-believer and his mother more interested in the pageantry of the Catholic Church than the spiritual aspects. The result was that soon after his Communion in 1936 he proclaimed himself an atheist. About this time he also became a voracious reader, a propensity he apparently inherited from his father. However, when he began devouring the works of such authors as Maugham, Huxley, Proust, Balzac, Tolstoy, Flaubert, Stendhal, and Hugo, the elder Donoso warned him against literature and predicted that it would be his undoing. José probably received his artistic nature from his mother, a highly imaginative woman whose stories and games provided a constant source of delight for her children.

In the late 1930's the Donoso family moved back to the house where José was born, and about this same time his maternal grandmother returned from Europe to make her home with them. The old lady's mental deterioration lasted for more than ten years, a drawn-out process which, in Donoso's words, "made life hell for us" and was "one of the episodes that has most marked my life . . . because her madness brought the ironies of family life and the horrors of aging and dying so cruelly into focus."[18]

The author's teenage years were not happy ones. A kind of rebel without a cause, he cut classes, continued to feign stomach-aches, spent entire days reading in the public library or wandering about the lower-class districts of Santiago and, when thrust into the approved middle-class world of young people's parties, "waged a brief but losing battle to belong."[19] In 1943 he dropped out of school and two years later, having been unable to hold a job for more than a few months, set out for Magallanes, the southern tip of Chile, where he worked on the pampas as a sheepherder for almost a year.[20] From Magallanes he hitchhiked through Patagonia to Buenos Aires where he supported himself as a dockhand and lived in a flophouse until he fell ill with a case of the measles and returned home.

In 1947 Donoso finished high school and enrolled in the Pedagogical Institute of the University of Chile, majoring in English, a career not generally approved of for an upper-middle-class youth. Two years later he received a scholarship to study at Princeton where he was awarded a B.A. degree but, in his own words, "turned out to be a very poor student."[21] Still, the years he spent at the prestigious American university (1949–1951) were to leave a lasting imprint on his life. He studied with several well-known literary scholars including R. P. Blackmur, Lawrence Thompson, and Allen Tate and discovered that a consuming interest in literature need not make one feel guilty, as he had been led to believe in Chile, but rather could be the source of legitimate pleasure. At Princeton he became fascinated with Henry James, whose works were being reappraised after a long period of neglect, and was introduced to the great paintings of the world, all of which was to influence his own writings. He also published his first two short stories, "The Poisoned Pastries" and "The Blue Woman" in *MSS*, a Princeton literary review.[22]

The period immediately following Donoso's return to Chile was, he believes, one of the most chaotic of his life.[23] He felt imprisoned in his native land, could not find a job to his liking, and his stomach pains, which had ceased in Magallanes and Princeton, came back with a vengeance, making it impossible for him to write. He underwent psychoanalysis for the first time and eventually began to teach English at the Catholic University and the Kent School in Santiago.

In 1954 "China," Donoso's first story written in Spanish, was included in an anthology of Chilean short fiction,[24] and the following year his first book, a collection of short stories entitled *Veraneo y otros cuentos* (Summertime and Other Stories) was published. It was well received by the critics, and won for its author the Santiago Municipal Short Story Prize. Encouraged by his success, Donoso set to work immediately on his first novel, *Coronación (Coronation)*, which he completed on Isla Negra, an island near the Chilean coast, where he lived with a fisherman's family. However, while riding a bus to take an advanced copy of his recently completed manuscript to a reviewer, he fainted from the effects of a hemorrhaging ulcer.

Although *Coronation* was highly acclaimed by the critics and sold well, Donoso soon began to tire of the oppressive atmosphere of upper-middle-class Chilean society and, carrying letters of introduction from the famous Chilean poet Pablo Neruda to literary pundits throughout the continent, set off on a tour of South America. He never went beyond Buenos Aires which he found so stimulating intellectually that he stayed almost two years. Another reason for his lengthy sojourn in the Argentine capital was his engagement to María del Pilar Serrano, the little girl from Antofagasta his English governess had gone to teach, now a sophisticated painter. They were married in 1961.

Upon his return to Santiago the previous year, Donoso had published his second collection of short stories, *El charleston (Charleston)*, and began a successful career as a journalist with the Chilean weekly news magazine *Ercilla*. He was awarded the Chile-Italia Prize for excellence in journalism and soon thereafter became the editor of *Ercilla* and the magazine's leading literary critic. During this period he also began lecturing in the School of Journalism at the University of Chile.

In 1965 Donoso signed a contract to teach in the Writers' Workshop at the University of Iowa, a position he held for two years. Even though he had many fine students and enjoyed his work, he discovered teaching and writing were incompatible, for whenever he tried to concentrate on what was to be his most ambitious novel to date. *El obsceno pájaro de la noche (The Obscene Bird of Night)*, his ulcer pains inevitably reappeared. He therefore decided to submit his resignation and move to Spain in order to finish the novel he had begun several years previously. The couple adopted an infant daughter in Madrid and settled in Mallorca where, in spite of their relatively peaceful life, Donoso's ailment still prevented him from writing. He suffered from hypochondria and once again sought the aid of a psychiatrist who, the author recalls, "for four months kept me only half awake, with barely any life at all in me except the vegetative. I was like a head of lettuce."[25]

Donoso received his first Guggenheim Award in 1968 but, realizing that he was unable to complete *The Obscene Bird of Night* at this time, he accepted an offer to lecture at Colorado State University for the winter quarter of 1969. After only two weeks of classes he fell dangerously ill with another hemorrhaging ulcer and was obliged to undergo surgery. For many hours after the operation he was delirious with hallucinations, split personality, paranoia, and suicide attempts stemming from his inability to tolerate morphine pain killers. As soon as he was able to travel, he flew back to Mallorca, moved his family to Barcelona, and although still suffering from the effects of his illness, began rewriting *The Obscene Bird of Night*, basing many passages of the book on his nightmarish experience in Colorado.

Once the novel was published, the Donosos began to look for a house outside of Barcelona so that José could recuperate from his months of exhausting work. In Calaceite, Teruel they bought a large seventeenth-century home, completely remodeled it, and in 1971 became residents of this charming village of approximately two thousand inhabitants. Since their move to Calaceite, two additional books by the author have appeared in print: *Historia personal del "boom" (The Boom in Spanish American Literature A Personal History)*, 1972, and *Tres novelitas burguesas (Sacred Families)*, 1973. During the summer of 1973 Donoso was awarded his second Guggenheim Fellowship to enable him to work on his next novel, *Casa de campo* (Country House). He was preparing to make his first trip to Chile in almost nine years when the September 11, 1973 military coup forced him to cancel his plans. Approximately two years later, however, he did visit his homeland, but he found the political climate so oppressive that he left, vowing never to return. Recently, Donoso moved his family to Sitges, a town near Barcelona, where he is finishing Country House.[26]

III *Donoso and the "Boom"*

During the 1960's the novel replaced poetry as the leading genre in contemporary Latin American literature. Because of the proliferation of fine prose fiction that occurred throughout the continent[27] during this period, critics began to speak of the so-called "boom," a literary phenomenon about which much has been written.[28] As the most outstanding Chilean novelist of his generation, Donoso played an important role in the boom during the 1960's, but it was not until the publication of *The Obscene Bird of Night* in 1970 that he was elevated to the highest ranks of contemporary Latin American novelists with Carlos Fuentes of Mexico, Gabriel García Márquez of Colombia, Mario Vargas Llosa of Peru, and Julio Cortázar of Argentina.

In reality the groundwork for the cultural atmosphere that gave rise to the boom was being laid for approximately two decades prior to the 1960's. In spite of the appearance of several outstanding Regionalist novels during the 1940's, by the beginning of the decade this literary form had, to quote Emir Rodríguez Monegal, "reached a dead end,"[29] and radical changes were necessary so that prose fiction would reflect more accurately the situation of modern man in the world. Latin America was beginning to industrialize, cities were growing, and cultured European World War II refugees were arriving who would contribute much to promote education and stimulate the publishing business. Intellectuals felt the impact of psychoanalysis and existentialism and, with the population explo-

sion and the construction of new schools and universities, the reading public began to expand. The following are some of the most
significant works of the 1940's which, by their fusion of objective
reality with fantasy, myth, surrealism or philosophical themes,
brought about the demise of Regionalist fiction and transformed the
literary scene: Adolfo Bioy Casares' *La invención de Morel* (The
Invention of Morel); Jorge Luis Borges' *Ficciones (Fictions)*; Miguel
Angel Asturias' *El señor Presidente (El Señor Presidente)*; Ernesto
Sábato's *El túnel (The Outsider)* and Alejo Carpentier's *El reino de
este mundo (The Kingdom of This World)*.

During the 1950's this new type of prose fiction, with its emphasis
on poetic invention and man's place in the universe, continued to
pave the way for the boom of the following decade with the publication of such works as Juan Carlos Onetti's *La vida breve (Brief Life)*
and *Los adioses (The Farewells)*; Alejo Carpentier's *Los pasos
perdidos (The Lost Steps)*; Carlos Fuentes' *La región más transparente (Where the Air is Clear)*; and José María Arguedas' *Los ríos
profundos* (The Deep Rivers). The most influential novel of this
decade, however, was Juan Rulfo's *Pedro Páramo (Pedro Páramo)*
after which, according to Emir Rodríguez Monegal, Latin American
fiction of the 1960's would branch out in three separate directions: 1)
the in-depth exploration of national realities; 2) the quest for the
realities revealed by myth; and 3) the experimentation with linguistic structures.[30]

Donoso's *The Boom in Spanish American Literature* . . . not only
lends insight into his development as a novelist, but also provides
information about the Chilean and Latin American literary scenes
during the 1950's and 1960's. According to Donoso, before 1960,
Chilean intellectuals of his generation were far more interested in
English, French, German, Italian, and American literatures than in
Spanish and other Latin American writers. They were well acquainted with the major Regionalist authors of the 1920's and
1930's, whom they had read in school, but they considered this
fiction simplistic, stereotyped, and fossilized. And until the late
1950's they were generally unaware of the new Latin American
writers such as Jorge Luis Borges, Alejo Carpentier and Juan Carlos
Onetti. In a sense, then, they regarded themselves as orphans in
their own countries where critics, publishers, and the reading public were still unwilling to accept new trends, especially in national
literature. Donoso believes, however, that this vacuum in which the

young authors found themselves had the healthful effect of inducing them to experiment with new forms and thus enrich their art.

The difficulties Latin American writers encountered in getting their works into print prior to the 1960's are illustrated by Donoso's efforts to find a publisher for his first books, *Veraneo y otros cuentos* and *Coronation*. Both were rejected by two firms before being accepted under rather unusual circumstances. Prior to its appearance *Veraneo y otros cuentos* was paid for by Donoso after which he, with the aid of his friends and members of his family, peddled copies on street corners and in bookstores to help defray expenses. *Coronation* was first rejected because it was considered too difficult for Chilean readers, a judgment that seems incredible today, and was finally published in an edition of three thousand copies with the stipulation that Donoso sell seven hundred as payment. Although *Veraneo y otros cuentos* won a prize for its author and *Coronation* was soon sold out, second editions were not even considered until several years later. Another problem confronting Latin American writers even as recently as the early 1960's was the deplorable fact that very few of their books were exported to other countries. This situation gave rise to what Donoso has labeled the *correo de chasquis* (mail service by Indian couriers), meaning that whenever authors traveled abroad they would inevitably carry suitcases bursting with books to distribute to their friends.

Donoso also discusses the well-known question of why so many prominent Latin American writers reside abroad today.[31] Rejecting the frequent criticism that authors living in self-imposed exile are escaping from, or simply ignoring, their national problems, he reminds his readers of the precedents set by the great Modernist poet from Nicaragua, Rubén Darío, who lived in Europe for many years early in the twentieth century, and by Neruda, Borges and the Peruvian poet César Vallejo, all residents of France and Spain during the 1920's and 1930's. There is obviously a wide variety of reasons for a group of writers to leave their native lands, but Donoso believes the causes are less political than psychological. In his own Latin American country, an outstanding writer is likely to be vilified and victimized in an atmosphere of petty jealousy, while once he has transcended national boundaries, he is more likely to encounter a spirit of camaraderie and intellectual exchange among men of letters. The appalling isolation of the author on his home soil, especially prior to the 1960's, emerges from *The Boom in Spanish Ameri-*

can Literature . . . as another probable reason for his quest for literary fortune in a more culturally stimulating environment.

In the late 1950's and early 1960's Donoso became acquainted with several recent Latin American novels that were to affect his aesthetic ideals and, consequently, his role in the boom. The first of these was Cuban author Alejo Carpentier's *The Lost Steps* which Donoso read in 1957 as he was finishing *Coronation.* The following quotation conveys his enthusiasm for the book and the great impact it had on him. "I devoured this novel at one sitting, reading day and night without stopping, and then I read it again while I rewrote my own novel. Perhaps, although in a very remote way, Carpentier's admirable contradiction of the rules of good taste that governed my thinking made possible the modest degree of freedom with which I treated the last part of *Coronation*, the style of which appeared to be, at the time, so far beyond Chilean tastes. I think that by pulling myself up to the level of *The Lost Steps*, for the first time I could see over the barriers that simplicity and realism had erected as the only destiny for our writings . . . in order to observe not only a much greater breadth but also dimensions not entirely beyond reach."[32]

The two years Donoso spent in Buenos Aires (1958–1960) were also to broaden his literary horizons, for it was here that he became acquainted with many important Argentine writers including Jorge Luis Borges, Beatriz Guido, David Viñas, Victoria Ocampo, Adolfo Bioy Casares, Silvina Bullrich, Ernesto Sábato, Mujica Lainez, and the Paraguayan novelist in exile, Augusto Roa Bastos. Here also Donoso was "dazzled" by his first reading of Borges' short stories, an experience reflected in his tale entitled "Pasos en la noche" ("Footsteps in the Night"). Regarding his visit to the Argentine capital, he concludes, "I had escaped from the cage and although I went back to Chile to live, I believe that after this trip to Buenos Aires my literary vision changed definitely."[33]

The year following Donoso's return to his native land he read Carlos Fuentes' *La región más transparente (Where the Air is Clear)*, a Mexican novel that perhaps had a greater impact on his literary orientation than any other single book he had read previously. Fuentes had utilized the latest technical procedures to compose a richly textured, satirical mosaic of post-revolutionary Mexican society and, at the same time, to examine in depth what it means to be a Mexican. Although the novel is often compared to John Dos Passos' *Manhattan Transfer* and the *U.S.A.* trilogy,

Donoso asserts correctly that whereas the American author's view of reality is documentary and coldly objective, Fuentes' is subjective and lyrical. It is precisely the Mexican author's "unbridled" subjectivity, together with his bold stylistic experimentation, spontaneous ambiguity, and provocative intellectual probings, that made Donoso change his entire concept of the novel and elicited from him the following comments: "Upon reading it [*Where the Air is Clear*] literature acquired another dimension because it abruptly wrenched me from the aesthetics in which, despite my trip to Buenos Aires, I was still imprisoned. In fact, on a more personal level, I believe it was this trauma—having wrenched myself from my traditional aesthetic points of view in order to acquire broader aesthetic ideals—that made it impossible for me to finish until many years later *The Obscene Bird of Night*, which had been conceived and perhaps begun about that time: it was, to put it simply, because of the terror of not being capable of fulfilling the literary demands that seemed so superior to those I had been accustomed to considering my own."[34]

"Perhaps the most profound impression caused by my reading of *Where the Air is Clear* was its non-acceptance, and rightly so, of a single unequivocal view of Mexican reality . . . Its attitude was not one of documentation, like that of the novelists who surrounded me in my own environment, but one of investigation."[35]

Donoso states further that European and American writers such as Joyce, Proust, D. H. Lawrence, Henry James, Faulkner, and Thomas Wolfe had influenced him by providing him with knowledge of literary theory and technique. However, whereas these authors had always seemed somewhat remote, Carlos Fuentes was a contemporary Spanish American who, by daring to overthrow sacred literary dogmas, had invaded Donoso's subjective world and inspired him to greater efforts. For the Chilean, "Reading *Where the Air is Clear* . . . was a vital impulse, a fierce incentive for my life as a writer, the inducement of envy, of a necessity to emulate which, combined with astonishment and admiration, ventilated my hermetic world."[36]

In 1962 both Donoso and Fuentes were invited to attend the Congress of Intellectuals at the University of Concepción, Chile, and when the Mexican writer arrived at the Santiago airport, Donoso was on hand to meet him with a copy of *Where the Air is Clear* which he hoped to have autographed. Fuentes also had studied at the Grange School in Santiago many years before (his

father was a diplomat) and immediately recalled that Donoso had
been several years ahead of him. Because of their mutual fear of
airplanes, they took the train to Concepción, thus having an opportunity to become better acquainted and to discuss the contemporary
Latin American literary and political scenes.[37] Donoso was not only
impressed by his friend's intellectual brilliance and flamboyant personality but also by his growing international reputation and numerous literary and political undertakings, all of which induced him to
write: "Looking back on things, as always, from my personal point
of view, Carlos Fuentes appears as the first conscious and active
agent for the internationalization of the Spanish American novel of
the 1960's."[38] Donoso views the meeting in Concepción as a mile-
stone in the genesis of the boom because, by providing a forum for
literary and political discussions, it helped to unify Latin American
intellectuals and make them more aware of the cultural revolution
being promoted by Cuba throughout the continent.[39] The confer-
ence also served to stimulate the desire for improved communica-
tions among Latin American writers, many of whom realized for the
first time that something important was occurring on their continent's literary scene. Still, even at this late date (1962), Donoso
recalls, the major Spanish American novelists of the 1940's and
1950's were only mentioned in passing, the reason being that their
works were still, for the most part, unavailable outside their own
countries. This cultural parochialism was about to change abruptly.

The same year as the congress in Concepción a Peruvian novel
entitled *La ciudad y los perros (The Time of the Hero)* was published in Spain by Editorial Seix Barral and awarded the Biblioteca
Breve Prize by the same firm. The appearance of this prize-winning
work, which electrified readers throughout the Spanish-speaking
world and became a best seller almost over night, quite possibly
marks the actual beginning of the boom.[40] In Donoso's opinion both
the novel's young author, Mario Vargas Llosa, and his publisher are
key figures in the boom, the former for his extraordinary achievement in revolutionary technique (Donoso was particularly impressed by the Peruvian's adroit manipulation of the point of view),
and the latter for the recognition and wide publicity he gave to this
and other avant-garde Latin American novels.[41] Indeed the financial
and literary success of *The Time of the Hero* was echoed by other
fine novels which, like the works of Carpentier, Fuentes, and Vargas
Llosa, were to have an influence on Donoso. The most important of

these was *Sobre héroes y tumbas* (About Heroes and Tombs), 1961, by the Argentine Ernesto Sábato, of which Donoso writes: ". . . this marvelous, uneven book fell into my hands just when I was obsessively writing and rewriting *The Obscene Bird of Night* for the purpose of discovering a rational form for the book. Just as *The Time of the Hero* freed me from the fetters that bound me to one single point of view within a novel, *Sobre héroes y tumbas* also appeared to be directed against my taboos, especially because it made me realize that to try to give rational form to something I was living as an obsession was a mistake . . . that the irrational could have the same, or even greater, significance than the rational and at times it can even disguise itself as rationality; that intelligence and irrationality are not contradictory words; that the irrational, the obsessive could have great literary importance, as Sábato gave it in *Sobre héroes y tumbas;* and that the phantoms of the irrational hide in everyday things and harass us with their concealed presences. That the rational, the intellectual, unmeasured and chaotic, can proliferate like a cancer and confer this unhealthy, cancerous atmosphere on a novel like *Sobre héroes y tumbas.*"[42]

Another important event that Donoso relates to the boom is the appearance in July, 1966 of a new literary journal entitled *Mundo Nuevo,* edited by Emir Rodríguez Monegal and sponsored by the Ford Foundation. Although the journal was boycotted from the beginning by Cuban intellectuals who suspected it was being subsidized by the CIA, it nevertheless, during the five years of its existence, published valuable critical studies on contemporary Latin American letters as well as excerpts of many fine novels prior to their appearance in final form. Donoso praises the journal in unequivocal terms. "During the years Emir Rodríguez Monegal directed it [1966–1968] this journal exercised a decisive role in defining a generation . . . *Mundo Nuevo* was the voice of the Latin American literature of its time, and for better or for worse . . . I am convinced that the history of the boom in the moment in which it reached its peak, is written in the pages of *Mundo Nuevo,* until the moment Emir Rodríguez Monegal gave up the editorship. Of all the literary journals of my time, from *Sur* to *Casa de las Américas,* . . . none has succeeded in conveying the enthusiasm for the existence of something alive in the literature of our time . . . with the precision and breadth of *Mundo Nuevo* during the last part of the 1960's."[43]

At the time of the Congress of Writers in Concepción, Carlos

Fuentes had strongly urged Donoso to send *Coronation* to Alfred A. Knopf to be considered for publication in English. Perhaps lacking confidence, Donoso did not take the matter seriously, but without his knowledge his wife mailed several copies of the novel to the New York firm, which in 1963 offered to publish it. This same year *Coronation* was selected by the Faulkner Foundation as the best Chilean novel written during the post-World War II period.

Because of Donoso's growing reputation both at home and abroad he was invited in December, 1964 to attend a symposium of writers organized by the Interamerican Foundation for the Arts and held in Chichén Itzá, Mexico. After the meetings, instead of returning to Chile as originally planned, he and his wife remained in Mexico City for several months where they lived in Carlos Fuentes' guest house. This sojourn in the Mexican capital proved to be a fruitful experience for, in addition to becoming acquainted with the city's intellectual community, Donoso completed *El lugar sin límites (Hell Has No Limits)* and much of *Este Domingo (This Sunday)*, both of which were published by one of Mexico's best publishing firms, Joaquín Mortiz. He also wrote literary commentaries for the journal *Siempre* and once found himself the center of much sympathetic attention when one of his articles belittling the Mexican novel appeared with a sentence appended in italics, "He's very good at criticizing, but he's a poor idiot."[44] The person who inserted the line remains anonymous to this day.

The boom reached its peak during the years 1965–1970 with the publication of Mario Vargas Llosa's *La casa verde (The Green House)*, 1965, and *Conversación en la Catedral (Conversation in the Cathedral)*, 1969; Carlos Fuentes' *Cambio de piel (Change of Skin)*, 1967; Gabriel García Márquez' *Cien años de soledad (One Hundred Years of Solitude)*, 1967; and Donoso's *The Obscene Bird of Night*, 1970. By the end of the decade, however, the term boom had begun to outlive its usefulness, partly because the word itself suggests an ephemeral impulse, and partly because, as Donoso elucidates in *The Boom in Spanish American Literature* . . . , three events occurred in late 1970 and early 1971 that had a dampening effect on the literary movement. The first of these was a controversy that split Seix Barral, the company which had played such a major role in fomenting the boom:[45] the second was the demise of the journal, *Mundo Nuevo;* and finally, the most dramatic event was the arrest of dissident Cuban poet Heberto Padilla by Fidel Castro's government, an action that created a furor among Latin American writers and shattered the decade-long unity of the leftist intellectual community.

Emir Rodríguez Monegal believes that although the boom is quite possibly dead, the new Latin American novel "is enjoying very good health."[46] Not only are most of the significant writers of the 1960's still alive and publishing, but a number of talented younger authors such as Argentina's Manuel Puig, Cuba's Severo Sarduy and Reynaldo Arenas, Peru's Alfredo Bryce Echeñique, Chile's Antonio Skármeta, and Mexico's Gustavo Sainz and José Agustín have emerged to swell their ranks. At the present time, while it is still difficult to arrange the past decade into the proper perspective, Donoso's concluding remarks on the boom offer a possible clue for future assessment. "The 'boom' has been a game; perhaps more precisely, a broth which for a decade nourished the outmoded form of the novel in Spanish America, and the ' boom ' will disappear—already it is spoken of less—and there will remain three or four or five outstanding novels which will remind us of it, and because of which all this noise and publicity will have been worthwhile."[47]

CHAPTER 2

The Short Stories

I Thematic Recurrences

ALTHOUGH Donoso is known primarily as a novelist, he has also published a total of seventeen short stories, all of which were written between 1950 and 1962.[1] These artistically drawn, psychologically penetrating studies of middle-class mores deserve critical acclaim for their intrinsic literary merit, but they are especially important here because they contain in embryonic form many of the thematic preoccupations developed at greater length in the novels.

"China," Donoso's first story written in Spanish, focuses nostalgically on the past as well as the inevitable loss of innocence and imagination that characterize adulthood. The mature protagonist-narrator recalls his fascination and delight when, as a child, he accompanied his mother to a lower-class section of the city one evening after a rain. As they walked along the noisy, brightly lighted street amidst the jostling crowds, his mother exclaimed, "Heavens, this is like China."[2] This remark, together with the exotic atmosphere, made such a strong impression on the child that soon thereafter he visited "China" again with his younger brother in tow. As time passed, he occasionally returned to the same district to browse through secondhand bookstores, but one day many years later, when he asked his brother where he might obtain a copy of a rare book, the reply, "In China," left him perplexed.

"Veraneo" (Summertime) also sets forth the loss-of-innocence theme, but even more important, it probes the complexities of human relationships and suggests the demise of one of man's most basic institutions, the family. The plot is sketched mainly through the actions and dialogues of adolescents and servants spending a summer at a beach resort. The nine-year-old protagonist, Raúl, makes friends with the more mature, domineering Jaime who introduces him to evil, symbolized by a slingshot, and orders him to laugh or weep according to which tune Jaime sings. Because of an affair between Jaime's mother and Raúl's father, the boys' friendship suddenly comes to an end and Raúl, now thoroughly dependent on Jaime, falls seriously ill. In the final scene the convalescent youngster, fully aware of his father's infidelity and displaying the unique mannerisms of his departed friend, is portrayed sitting alone on the beach staring toward the horizon.

Domination, dependence, and the fusion of identities in "Summertime," though important, are overshadowed by another theme which recurs in many of Donoso's subsequent works and which is introduced here in the form of a house symbol. Referred to repeatedly as "the palace," the edifice becomes a leitmotif that is eventually described in detail.

It was on top of a small sand dune. It had been, perhaps at the beginning of the century, a large wooden mansion, with a main entrance hall and two small towers in front, facing the sea. But little remained of the structure. For years the birds had built their nests among its lead-colored beams, flying through what had been its dining room, living room and bedrooms. It was only a skeleton. It probably had been abandoned for at least thirty years . . . during which time the need of poor people to keep warm had deprived it of its doors, windows and walls and the disloyalties in taste and fashion had transformed it into something ridiculous. But absurd, poor, useless as it was, it had been rescued by the compassion of those children who, living in clean, modern houses in the nearby resort, had detected in it a colorful legend. In the windows of the little towers . . . there remained some pieces of colored glass . . . In the afternoon, the magic hour for the palace, the sun's rays broke on the remaining pieces of glass. Then, fleetingly, the two towers glowed with glory, breaking the light into a thousand flashes and flooding the melancholy skeleton of the house in shadows. (p. 35)

An integral part of the plot, this dilapidated house symbolizes the "false family," a term Donoso uses to indicate a negation of the archetypal, close-knit family unit, which has been eroded by time, infidelity, and hypocrisy. The decaying structure also conveys, through magical moments of beauty, the nostalgia for childlike innocence, imagination, and delight that emerged from "China" and that will make its final appearance in *This Sunday*.

"Ana María" presents another interpretation of the false-family and fusion-of-identity motifs. Here an impoverished old man and his

barren wife have given up all pretense of love after thirty years of
marriage while, at the other extreme, a young couple with a three-
year-old daughter, Ana María, are interested solely in sex. Left to
wander aimlessly through a densely wooded garden, the child becomes friendly with the old man who works on a construction site
nearby. When the latter finds himself unemployed and abandoned
by his embittered spouse, he goes to bid the child a fond farewell.
However, upon being confronted with her beautiful, hypnotic eyes,
he offers no resistance as she leads him away to an uncertain
destiny.

The bonds of friendship between the old man and Ana María
result from their mutual loneliness and illustrate Donoso's belief in
the magnetic attraction often felt between unlike human beings.[3]
Their unique relationship, which anticipates the kind of symbiotic
unions evidenced in some of the author's future works,[4] also derives
from Ana María's aura of innocence, her instinctual behavior,[5] and
her "deep eyes, shining stealthily among the branches," (p. 197) all
of which leads to the poignant denouement.

"Dos cartas" (Two Letters), albeit one of Donoso's least distin-
guished pieces of short fiction, touches on a theme that assumes
major proportions in much of his subsequent literary production,
i.e., Chile's rigidly stratified social structure which imprisons the
middle and upper classes in a stifling atmosphere of conformity.
One of the protagonists of "Dos cartas" is a young Chilean lawyer
named Jaime Martínez who approaches the pinnacle of success in
his profession with the uneasy awareness that his family's prominent
position "has made him a prisoner without giving him stability" and
that "he had not chosen his profession and way of life but rather . . .
they were imposed on him and therefore he was a prisoner of dissatisfaction and anxiety." (p. 114) After confessing his anguish and
frustration in a letter to a former college friend, he decides to destroy what he has written because "he found it incoherent, senti-
mental, literary, revealing a part of himself that, after all, had not
really had any major importance in determining his destiny." (p.
117) In the case of Martínez, the strict adherence to conventional
behavior, the excessive stress on the so-called rational side of life
and the suppression of all emotions bordering on the irrational
merely inflate his conscious ego and enhance his professional success. In Donoso's best fiction, however, the darker, instinctive side
of existence surges forth and either alters or controls the destiny of
his characters.

This is precisely what occurs in "El güero" (The Güero) a tale that takes place in a tropical Mexican village, Tlacotlalpan, where an American professor of botany (Mr. Howland), his wife (also a botanist), and their blond, nine-year-old son Mike live for an extended period of time. Mrs. Howland describes herself and her husband as "the kind of people who live according to theories, theories that stipulate the precise name and the exact weight of everything, thus rejecting all possibility of mystery." (p. 62) Their son, whom Mrs. Howland considers a perfect specimen of innocence, intelligence, and beauty, has never attended school prior to their arrival in Tlacotlalpan, having been educated solely by his parents so that he could "reason for himself and act according to his inclinations, free from all the dark forces that might dull what was to be the fullest of lives." (p. 65)

The family rents a house from a vivacious, superstitious, Indian woman named Amada Vásquez[6] who serves as their housekeeper and fascinates Mike with her tales of powerful, pale-skinned gods living at the source of the nearby river. Meanwhile Mike attends school and soon begins to dominate his classmates who consider him the embodiment of one of the blond gods. Alarmed at this turn of events, Mrs. Howland observes

the change that took place in Mike during our stay in Tlacotlalpan, in contact with so much primitive energy, in the presence of Amada and those children whose eyes were acquainted with the ancient vocabulary of the jungle and the river. Mike himself was like a river that had overflowed its banks from heavy rains. All the forces seemed to have spilled over within my son and as I was blind, I didn't realize that he was too fragile to endure the weight of these forces. I say blind because I had faith that the contact with Mike would serve as a civilizing element for those children, since not only for me, but also for them, he was a superior being. I didn't know that they and everything that surrounded them had expanded Mike's life to the point that all the mystery and everything that vibrates with hidden force had become a natural part of his being. (p. 74)

The tale reaches its climax with a tropical storm during which Mike and a select group of his friends embark in a boat and are drowned upon trying to reach the abode of the legendary gods. This tragic event has a renovating effect on the Howlands whose narrow rationalism is henceforth tempered by a broader understanding of themselves and the instinctual world around them. As Mrs. Howland concludes,

I hated that town, those people. But little by little I saw things more clearly
and discovered a new love for my work, for my husband and for people. I
had time to think a lot and to trace, so to speak, a line around what had
happened. But not a line that separated it from my life and from the rest of
human experiences . . . (pp. 77–78)

The dichotomy between the rational and the instinctual spheres
of the mind is nowhere more evident in Donoso's works than in
"Paseo,"[7] perhaps his finest story. The protagonist, an unattractive,
strait-laced spinster named Mathilda, supervises the household of
her three brothers, all of whom are successful lawyers in an un-
named port city.[8] The strictly, indeed fanatically, observed routine
of their existence is interrupted by the appearance of a white, mongrel bitch that follows Mathilda home from Mass on a rainy day and
little by little wins her affection. One night she takes the dog for a
walk and never returns.

An outstanding artistic achievement more than anything else,
"Paseo" immerses its reader into a fictional realm fraught with irony
and contrapuntal overtones fluctuating between rigid logic and terrifying ambiguity. This story also represents a focal point in
Donoso's total literary production because of the fact that its social
and psychological implications become obsessions in the novels.
The Chilean author's excessively rational middle-and upper-class
characters generally lead sterile, routine lives, suffer from varying
degrees of neuroses, and often depend on their contacts with the
more instinctive and sexually vigorous lower classes for infusions of
vitality. This marked difference in character traits between classes
recalls Freud's contentions that culture results from the repression
of instincts, that neurosis is a necessary product of culture, and that
the higher the culture the higher the degree of repression and
neurosis.[9] In "Paseo" much stress is placed on the characters' lack of
spontaneous affection for each other and their resulting isolation.

There was something rigid in her [Mathilda's] affections, as there was in
those of the men of the family. With them, love existed confined inside each
individual, never breaking its boundaries to express itself and bring them
together. For them to show affection was to discharge their duties to each
other perfectly, and above all not to inconvenience, never to inconvenience . . .[10]

Mathilda's conversations with her young nephew, her widowed
brother's son and the story's witness-narrator, reveal her unaware-

ness of the instinctual aspects of life and her contempt for anything beyond the borders of their narrowly circumscribed existence:

> She spoke to me about her brothers' integrity as lawyers in the intricate field of maritime law, and she extended to me her enthusiasm for their wealth and reputation, which I would carry forward. She described the embargo on a shipment of oranges, told of certain damages caused by miserable tugboats manned by drunkards, of the disastrous effects that arose from the demurrage of a ship sailing under an exotic flag. But when she talked to me of ships her words did not evoke the hoarse sounds of ships' sirens that I heard in the distance on summer nights when, kept awake by the heat, I climbed to the attic, and from an open window watched the far off floating lights, and those blocks of darkness surrounding the city that lay forever out of reach for me because my life was, and would ever be, ordered perfectly. I realize now that Aunt Mathilda did not hint at this magic because she did not know of it. (p. 311)

The protagonist's attitude toward mestizos emerges when a dark-complected man on the street greets her without tipping his hat and she expresses her surprise that "someone of mixed blood had bowed to her with so little show of attention . . . ." (p. 314) As far as animals are concerned, for Mathilda and her brothers they "existed only in the proportion in which they contributed to the pleasure of human beings. Which is to say that dogs . . . could not even dent their imagination with a possibility of their existence." (p. 313)

The rigidity of the characters' lives is also manifested in their daily routines such as the ritualistic game of billiards they play each night after dinner. The narrator recalls how he would wish that just once his father would rebel against the order of the game established by Mathilda, but that "this order was in itself a kind of rebellion, constructed by them as a protection against chaos, so that they might not be touched by what can be neither explained nor resolved." (pp. 312–13) This desire to shut out the dangers of the unknown is also reflected in Mathilda's metaphysical convictions to which the young narrator reacts with enthusiasm. "I exulted at the world of security that her words projected for me, that magnificent straight road which leads to a death that is not dreaded since it is exactly like this life, without anything fortuitous or unexpected. Because death was not terrible. Death was the final incision, clean and definitive, nothing more." (p. 311) And one day upon leaving church his aunt informs him that death is "the good foreseen end," that the purpose of masses, novenas and communions is to pray "that it [death] might not be painful." (p. 314)

Donoso is of the opinion that daily routine carried to excess constitutes false rituals which substitute meaningless activity for living and, as suggested by the preceding quotations, bring death into life in order to eliminate the terror of nothingness.[11] Routine activity and strict, rational behavior in "Paseo" not only isolate the characters from each other but, in the case of Mathilda, make her vulnerable to the mysterious forces of life she has always suppressed. Her strange behavior and ultimate disappearance evoke elements of the psychology of Carl G. Jung who, like Freud, has attributed many of modern man's neuroses to the split or "dissociation" of his rational conscious from the darker, unconscious levels of his psyche. In the interest of mental health Jung stresses the necessity of keeping channels open between these two spheres of the human mind in order to overcome the emotional imbalance caused by twentieth-century man's overdeveloped rational consciousness. This dangerous lopsidedness, Jung believes, leaves the individual powerless in the face of the raw instinctual energy likely to burst forth at any moment from the stifled unconscious and express itself in the form of symbolic images and neurotic behavior.[12]

In Donoso's works symbols frequently become obsessions that take hold of his excessively rationalistic characters and little by little consume them. The mongrel bitch in "Paseo," for example, whose "genealogy of misalliances" (p. 314) and "tail . . . curled up like a feather, leaving her shameless bottom in plain view" (p. 318) would seem to embody Mathilda's repressed instincts, a call to adventure given in response to her overpowering unconscious needs. Indeed, when she first meets the dog and turns suddenly to send it on its way, the look that passes between them appears to contain a "secret commitment" and Mathilda's "peremptory 'psst' had the sound of something like a last effort to repel an encroaching destiny." (p. 315) Some days later the family's solemn routines and rituals are disrupted by the bitch's mysterious appearance in the vestibule which elicits Mathilda's vow to treat her cuts and fever. Soon thereafter the dog accompanies her mistress into the billiard room where, "obeying an instinct that seemed to surge up from her picaresque past" (p. 319), she snatches a piece of chalk from one of Mathilda's brothers and,

Aunt Mathilda, as if suddenly unwound, burst into a peal of laughter that agitated her whole body. We remained frozen . . . the bitch dropped the chalk, . . . and jumped up onto her lap . . . now it was more important than ever not to see, not to see anything at all, not to comment, not to consider oneself alluded to by these events. (p. 319)

Nor does the young narrator find his aunt's laugh amusing because "I may have felt the dark thing that had stirred it up." (p. 319) He also notices that when Mathilda's hand comes to rest on her pet's back, the tension in her features disappears and "a certain peace was now softening her face." (p. 320)

As the days pass "the entwining relationship" (p. 320) between the white bitch and her mistress becomes increasingly evident until one evening an embarrassing puddle is discovered in the door of the billiard room and Mathilda initiates their nightly outings. The narrator soon realizes that

she was no longer a woman taking her dog out for hygienic reasons: outside there, in the streets of the city, something was drawing her . . . Those two were accomplices. The night protected them. They belonged to the murmuring sound of the city, to the sirens of the ships which . . . reached my ears. (pp. 322–23)

Once when Mathilda returns with the dog in her arms "her face seemed to me surprisingly young and unblemished, even though it was dirty, and I saw a rip in her skirt. I went to bed terrified, knowing this was the end." (pp. 323–24) A short time thereafter she leaves the house, never to be seen again.

"Paseo" sets forth what might be considered a classical existential situation, on the one hand a perfectly ordered, seemingly placid life and, on the other, a crisis which erupts with diabolical force, stifling reason and submerging the individual into an abyss created by his—in this case her—own obsessions. Mathilda's alienation from the instinctual inner self makes her not only a casualty of the illness Jung has diagnosed in his analysis of the contemporary psyche, but also a precursor of the obsessed, irrational figures populating Donoso's subsequent fiction.[13]

A somewhat similar existential crisis dominates "El charleston" (Charleston) in which three carefree young men, close friends since childhood, spend their leisure hours drinking wine and discussing

sports and amusing escapades with women. One evening after a
movie they enter a bar where they watch a drunken fat man play a
juke box and frenetically dance the Charleston. Suddenly he col-
lapses and writhes on the floor in agony until he loses consciousness
and probably dies.[14] This abrupt suggestion of death strikes terror
into the hearts of the three youths who remain separated for almost
two weeks before resuming their drinking bouts.

Like "Paseo," "Charleston" depicts characters whose fanatical
dedication to routine structures their lives, provides a barrier
against the unknown, and creates an illusion of eternal happiness.
Several statements of the narrator (one of the three protagonists)
indicates the ritualistic nature of their daily existence:

At times I think life would really be sad without friends to enjoy and drink
wine with from time to time . . . . (p. 137) I don't know if anybody has
thought about what a good thing football is for making friends—you go to
the games with friends, buy sports magazines with pictures of the players
and have something to talk about for weeks on end. Actually it fills up your
life . . . . (p. 138) Yes, that's the way it is. Your bottles of wine on the table
of a bar, your hot beef sandwich so as not to drink on an empty stomach,
your good cigarettes, friends ready to have a good time together . . . and
you go on talking and talking, drinking and drinking, and hours pass without
your realizing it until two, three, four o'clock in the morning. (p. 142)

The young men's false sense of security becomes evident when,
confronted by the existential void in the form of the agonizing fat
man, they succumb to feelings of anxiety and irrational hostility
toward each other. Thus, after leaving the bar that night, the narrator recalls, "we didn't even look at each other to say goodbye.
Maybe they also hated me at that moment," (p. 148) and during the
days immediately following he avoids his friends because

it occurred to me, I don't know why, that they were to blame for everything
that had happened that night. And all the fear I felt when I thought about the
fat man—because I was afraid, I have no reson to deny it—would be much
worse if I saw them again, because we'd start drinking again and I didn't feel
like it. (p. 149)

Gradually, however, the terror of aloneness looms greater than that
of death and, in order to suppress their anxiety, the three friends
renew their ritualistic camaraderie in the following manner. Thir-

teen days after the tragic event they meet by chance in the neighborhood and agree to attend a movie together that night. As they return home in unaccustomed silence, it occurs to the narrator that if they do not enter the last bar on their route, it will probably mean the end of their friendship.

> But upon arriving at the door of the bar we all three stopped at the same time. I looked at Jaime and at Memo and I realized that they also had thought the same thing I had. And when the three of us, standing there, burst out laughing simultaneously, we knew the danger had passed. (p. 150)

What they do not realize, however, is that the routine they are about to resume in reality represents a form of self-evasion, a means of warding off the fear of nothingness and concealing the absurdity of their human condition.[15]

Another of Donoso's finest stories is "Santelices," a carefully constructed and compelling psychological sketch of a sadomasochist whose neurotic expressions of anxiety and hostility eventually lead to the complete dissolution of his personality. Santelices is a shy, insignificant office clerk living in a drab boarding house owned by Doña Berta and her aging father, Don Eusebio. One of his few pleasures in life is looking at his collection of pictures of wild animals which, because of their beauty, strength, and ferocity, provide him with moments of relief from his monotonous daily routine. Tacked on the walls of Santelices' room, these pictures are accidentally discovered by Don Eusebio and, much to the boarder's chagrin and resentment, taken from him. A short time later Santelices sees from his office window a girl playing with a cat in a garden-patio five stories below. In his imagination this animal gives birth to a litter of kittens which, observed daily through field glasses, multiplies fantastically, in the end becoming a horde of wild beasts. Santelices' torment ceases when he leaps from the window into the garden, ostensibly to save the girl from danger.

The protagonist's neurotic anxiety and hostility are manifested by his strange reactions to the pictures with which he identifies as both aggressor and victim.

> Here in the sensational photographs which he looked at with the back of his neck cold from emotion, the proximity of danger, the naked cruelty, appeared to increase the beauty, endow it with an overwhelming force, mak-

ing it boil, flame, dazzle, and even leave his hands perspiring and his
eyelids fluttering. (p. 265) . . . In the twilight of his room . . . he would
look at the pictures, search for his emotion lost among the illustrations
which remained perversely inanimate, reduced to paper and ink
prints . . . . The avidity of his search crippled his imagination because the
yearning to obtain that precise thing grew like a blinding and paralyzing
vine which left space for nothing but itself. (p. 265)

One day Santelices visits the zoo where he watches the wild animals
eat red chunks of meat "making the bones crack, growling and
dripping hot saliva as they devoured them." (p. 266) This experience, however, leaves him dissatisfied with his beautiful pictures in
which the beasts' "triangular smile" and "sinuous walk" previously
had provided a satisfactory "insinuation of death."

Hungrily he looked for ferocious scenes in which the reality of steaming
fauces would be dyed with the ardor of blood, or in which the weight of the
animal would let fall all its brutality on the terrified victim. Santelices'
heart would beat together with the victim's, and in order to save himself from
panic he would fix his eyes on the aggressor in order to identify himself with
him. (p. 266)

Prior to the discovery of his collection, Santelices' relationship
with Doña Berta had been one of mild dependence and domination.
The middle-aged spinster had, for example, taken care of him after
his ulcer operation and insisted that he occupy a room next to hers
when he would have preferred to be left alone to pursue his hobby.
Considering him like one of the family, she also cooks his favorite
dishes and mends his clothes. However, when the escape valve for
Santelices' fluctuating emotions is shut off by the removal of his
pictures, a more intense, dialectical relationship between the two
characters rapidly develops.[16]
    At first Santelices is made to feel humiliated by the incident
involving his photos when Doña Berta scolds him and then tearfully
accuses him of ingratitude. He reacts by fleeing to his office from
where, for the first time, he catches sight of the girl and her cat in
the garden-patio. For several days he fearfully avoids any contact
with Doña Berta, all the time longing to return to the security of
their previous relationship which he subconsciously sees reflected
in the girl (Doña Berta) and her cat (Santelices' suppressed ego). The
birth of the cat's five or six kittens provides him with the courage he

needs to face Doña Berta again and resume his routine existence. However, still smarting from the loss of his collection, he soon begins to imagine that the girl in the garden, instead of playing with five or six kittens, is surrounded by numerous treacherous-looking felines. A reflection of his growing resentment, this hallucination triggers his complaint about a meal Doña Berta has served as well as his demand to know what she has done with his pictures. Her evasive reply and admission that she has framed one of them to hang in her room infuriates Santelices and precipitates the tragic denouement. In his fevered imagination, the cats become ferocious beasts embodying his wrath, and the girl, onto whom he projects his terror, assumes the role of imminent victim. His dramatic leap would therefore seem to represent a simultaneous expression of both his aggressive and self-destructive tendencies, a sadomasochist's dual attempt to evade his unbearable reality. The immediate impact of this story's probings into the obscure realm of human passions is enhanced by the disturbing social, psychological, and philosophical implications which figure prominently in most of Donoso's subsequent works.[17]

"Fiesta en grande" (Celebration on a Grand Scale) has many elements in common with "Santelices" including its central theme of domination and dependence. Alberto Aldea is a timid, middle-aged, office clerk who, like Santelices, makes his home in a boarding house. The day after he wins the national pistol shooting championship, his office colleagues (Freddie, Martita, and Elvira) plan a picnic in his honor to celebrate the occasion. While they are relaxing under a willow tree in the country, Alberto and Freddie suddenly become embroiled in a quarrel over a remark made by the latter about Martita. Wearing a ridiculous Napoleon hat and declaring his intention of defending the lady's honor, Alberto rushes toward Freddie with his pistol raised but trips and falls, causing the weapon to discharge. Thoroughly humiliated, he rides home alone in the back seat of the car, retires immediately, and has a dream with strong Freudian overtones. While he is asleep his domineering mother removes his pistol from his jacket, intending to dispose of it the following day. In the final scene Alberto awakens momentarily and begs his mother not to leave him alone until he falls asleep.

Despite its well drawn characters, "Fiesta en grande" leans too heavily on irony and suffers from an excess of Freudian symbolism. The theme of maternal castration would have been less obvious, and thus more effective, had the story ended with Alberto's dream which succinctly conveys his repressed hostility and pathetic destiny. Moments before falling asleep he is vaguely aware of sword-shaped rays of light entering through cracks in the door and of the noises made by his mother as she limps about in the next room, "always putting things in order." (p. 103) In his dream Alberto pursues a willow tree wearing a lilac-colored kerchief (like the one Martita wore around her neck), duals with a man resembling Napoleon (an identity he projects onto Freddie), and ultimately pierces the willow tree with his sword (a phallic symbol) just before a group of limping policemen come to arrest him. This Surrealistic nightmare reiterates the crippling effects of domination but, perhaps more significantly, represents an early example of Donoso's fascination with the subconscious.

Another example of surrealism in Donoso's short fiction is "Una señora" ("A Lady") which presents the Freudian will-to-kill obsession and, simultaneously, exposes the dark side of the psyche. While riding a streetcar one day, the narrator sits briefly next to an ordinary looking, middle-aged woman in a green raincoat. The next evening he is convinced he catches sight of the same person again and, during the following weeks, imagines he meets her frequently on the street. When he does not see her for some time, he begins to search for her obsessively and even falls ill from thinking about her. One morning he awakens certain that somewhere in the city she is dying and that evening, when all the noises of the neighborhood suddenly cease, he feels equally certain of her death. The next day he follows the funeral procession of a woman whose demise he has seen announced in the newspaper and, after the burial service, takes a stroll through the cemetery, feeling strangely at peace with himself. This ending, by means of which the narrator imposes his subjective interpretation of the world on objective reality, suggests the surrealists' attempt to break through the outer limits of the rational consciousness in order to discover a more comprehensive "surreality."[18]

The author's preoccupation with the nature of reality, including its metaphysical aspects, is perhaps best expressed in his short fiction by his most enigmatic tale, "La puerta cerrada" ("The Closed Door"). The setting, like that of the two preceding stories, is a boarding house and home for a false family, in this case a young widow and her son Sebastián Rengifo. Sebastián is considered odd because of his inordinate fondness for sleeping, an activity that leaves him no time for normal relations with other people. He confesses that he always dreams of a magical world of light, truth, and happiness but that as soon as he awakens a door shuts out what he has just envisioned. His overriding ambition is to open the door so that he can fuse his dream world with everyday reality. In the office where he is employed his supervisor, Aquiles Marambio, predicts a bright future for him but advises him to be more outgoing with his co-workers in order to improve his professional prospects. Sebastián informs Aquiles that he prefers sleeping to socializing and explains his preoccupation with the closed door. Although Aquiles scoffs at him, their discussion leads to a bet that when Sebastián dies, if he has a smile on his face—an indication that he has been able to open the door—Aquiles will pay for his funeral. Upon the death of his mother, Sebastián immediately resigns from his position in order to spend his time sleeping. Years later, impoverished, ostracized, and still striving to realize his ambition, he is overtaken by death at the entrance to Aquiles' home. Because of the radiant smile on his face, his former supervisor feels obliged to defray his funeral expenses.

The principal questions raised by this tale are what, if anything, the protagonist, the closed door, and the world beyond it represent. Sebastián evokes the sensitive, imaginative dreamer whose rejection of conventional values sets him apart from his fellow men. His role as an outsider becomes even more apparent when Aquiles rails at him for resigning from his position to devote himself to his favorite occupation. "Don't come to me with your nonsense about visions. The truth of the matter is that you're lazy, like all you people who consider yourselves select spirits. What gives you the right to a life of privileges?" (p. 169)

Sebastián's striving to open the door also recalls the surrealists' ideal of achieving a total reality by erasing the line between the real and the imaginary, an ideal illustrated by his desire "to bring the happiness of his dream world into this life, into this reality," (p. 160) and his gradual feeling that "the distance which formerly separated 'everyday reality' from the other reality, the more truthful one, was being shortened, because it seemed to him that all the rich exterior world was being incorporated into the hidden reality of the dream." (p. 171)

In view of his isolation, sensitivity, and obsessive efforts to unveil a perfect, all-encompassing reality, Sebastián also brings to mind the dedicated artist whose lifelong search for beauty becomes a metaphor of modern man's quest for the missing God.[19] Thus, he is convinced that opening the door would "provide him . . . powerful weapons . . . rich immense things with which he, Sebastián Rengifo, would somehow make the edge of darkness recede." (p. 170)

The religious fervor of his endeavor is again implied at the end of the story when, upon returning from church, Marambio Aquiles' young daughters discover Sebastián's body in the doorway of their home. At first they are frightened by the sight of death, but then the serenely happy expression on his face elicits the following exchange:

"Look, Daddy, how beautiful! It looks as if he had seen. . ."
"Shut up, don't say such stupid things!" exclaimed Marambio, furious.
"It looks as though he were seeing . . ." (p. 179)

But before they can say anything more, Marambio pushes them into the house and closes the door.

The little girls' suggestion that Sebastián has seen God may be much closer to the truth than their philistine father is capable of imagining, for if artistic perfection does indeed constitute Sebastián's concept of God, the smile on his face would seem to indicate that the moment of death became for him the supreme moment of aesthetic revelation, i.e., the moment in which he at last achieved the absolute beauty or the total reality he had sought all his life.[20] The closed door, then, symbolizes not only the insurmountable barrier between objective reality and subjective art, but also the separation between society and the artist. Whatever its interpretation, "The Closed Door" stands out as one of Donoso's most significant and fascinating tales. Its harmoniously fused singleness of action and multiplicity of suggestion anticipate the combination of unity and complexity so characteristic of his novels.

II *Irony in Donoso's Short Stories*

Irony has played an increasingly significant role in modern literature, particularly in the present century, and because of its complex, multifaceted, and elusive nature, it has become one of the most controversial concepts in aesthetics. Verbal irony has been defined as saying one thing and meaning another, but irony can also be situational, in which case it involves the occurrence of the unexpected or the incongruous, often at the expense of a confident, unwary victim. Irony frequently stems from the contrast between appearance and reality as presented by a detached observer who tends to look down on his subject with a combination of amusement and superiority. The juxtaposition of opposites also characterizes much ironic literature, its purpose being not only to reveal the contradictions and incongruities in the world, but also to enhance the aesthetic elements of balance and ambiguity.[21]

Donoso, like many contemporary writers, utilizes irony as a means of coming to grips with, and asserting a measure of independence from, a paradoxical world devoid of absolutes. Virtually all of the Chilean author's short stories contain elements of irony, but in several it emerges as a basic ingredient and in one, "Fiesta en grande," its omnipresence becomes oppressive and constitutes a flaw. This tragicomedy's situational irony stems from the contradictions between the protagonist's high aspirations and the cruel blows of fate that lie in store for him. In the opening scene Alberto Aldea, sporting a flashy new necktie, eagerly awaits the opportune moment to impress his office colleagues with the news of his pistol-shooting championship. Their enthusiastic invitation to celebrate his triumph contrasts sharply with the descriptions of his drab home life and his anxiety, generated by timidity, over the thought of a fiesta. His moments of prestige come to an abrupt end during the absurd incident in the country after which his domineering mother confiscates his pistol with the intention of throwing it into the river on her way to Mass the next day. Alberto's dream, replete with Freudian symbols, and his resultant terror of being left alone without his mother complete the annihilation of his illusions and, perhaps, of his entire personality. The end result of this accumulation of ironic events is an excess of cruelty that transforms farce into tragedy and amusement into exaggerated pathos.

In "Charleston" Donoso successfully conveys a strong sense of irony by telling his tale of the dancing fat man in the words of his naive protagonist whose confident unawareness of his situation serves to conceal the author's purpose and relegates to the reader the discovery of any ironic intent. The narrator and his two friends emerge as victims of irony because, when they find themselves suddenly overwhelmed by the terror of death, they fail to discern the cause of their irrational hostility toward one another, thus creating a gulf between themselves and the more perspicacious reader. The latter's distance and objectivity enable him to sense by intuition the metaphysical reality of their situation, i.e., that the fat

man's ridiculous antics and abrupt confrontation with death constitute a frightening symbol of the absurd.[22] Irony is merely enhanced
at the end of the story when the three youths resume their drinking
rituals without ever suspecting the profound existential nature of
their experience. The subtle interplay in "Charleston" between appearance and reality tends to modify opposites and raise questions
regarding the uncommitted author's attitude toward his characters.
Does he, like his reader, view the unsuspecting "victims" with
ironic detachment, or does he consider the three youths all the
wiser to forget about the fat man and hold on to their comforting
illusions?

Donoso's most ambiguous short story, "The Closed Door," also
exposes disconcerting aspects of the human condition. A high degree of ironic detachment is achieved in both this tale and "Charleston," but whereas in the latter the author wears the disguise of an
ingenuous first-person narrator, in the former he relates the sequence of events in the third person, maintaining narrative distance
through strict objectivity. The leading figures of "The Closed Door"
are social and psychological opposites, Sebastián representing the
subjective artist and Aquiles, the rationally oriented materialist.
Still, these characters have one important thing in common: both
think in terms of absolutes. Sebastián labors under the illusion that
truth, beauty, and omnipotence are within his grasp, and Aquiles is
thoroughly convinced that he has already discovered the ultimate in
human values. Their ignorance of the absurdity of their situations
contrasted with the reader's amused awareness of their futile en-
tanglements makes them both victims of metaphysical irony. Sebastián's idealism and naiveté prevent him from actively participating
in life and leave him vulnerable to the cruel reality that only in
death do man's expectations cease to be frustrated. Thus, when he
dies with the same smile he wore in his sleep, one can speculate that
perhaps his obsessive search for the unattainable was in reality an
attempt to avoid the pitfalls of life by replacing it with a passive state
akin to death. On the other hand, Aquiles' stubborn refusal to admit
the possibility of Sebastián's success in opening the door casts doubt
on the validity of his (Aquiles') narrow philosophical horizons.
Sebastián wins the bet and, more than likely, the reader's sym-
pathy, but from the viewpoint of the ironic observer, the situation of
both men could be considered absurd. The ironically aloof author
not only sets forth the clash between human aspirations and death

but also juggles opposites and balances possibilities all of which tends to invalidate incompatible points of view and deny the existence of any standard for moral behavior.

In "A Lady," the tale about the woman in the green raincoat, Donoso once again achieves distance and irony, this time by telling his tale in the words of a neurotic, first-person narrator who candidly describes his preoccupation with the woman, her imagined death, and his return to "normality." The protagonist emerges as a victim of irony because he is so utterly oblivious to his will-to-kill instinct which little by little takes possession of his psyche and eventually puts an end to his strange obsession. The contrast between his intense emotional involvement and the reader's intellectual comprehension creates a tension which is reinforced by the descriptions of exterior reality as interpreted by the protagonist's fluctuating states of mind. For example, just before his will to destroy reaches the stage of physical illness, he visits an ugly plaza with withered trees and a littered fountain falling in ruins, while on the day he imagines the woman is dying the air seems to sparkle with pleasant, distinctly audible sounds. Then unexpectedly

all the noises stopped at the same time and utter silence ensued. The wires ceased to vibrate. In an unknown district of the city the woman had died. . . . The afternoon came to an imperceptible end as my thoughts about the woman were gradually extinguished.

And after the funeral: "I walked for awhile under the dark trees because that sunny afternoon I felt especially calm." (pp. 86–87) Thus, the narrator molds the contours of the objective world to suit his shifting moods, resulting in a montage of clashing images that illuminate the subjective nature of reality and make ambiguity a balancing as well as an aesthetic ingredient.

Donoso's masterpiece of irony in his short fiction is "Paseo," the tale of the middle-aged spinster who disappears while walking her dog. This story differs from the others discussed in that it utilizes verbal as well as situational irony, i.e., the words themselves, in addition to the occurrences, convey a duality of meaning. Here a point of view is adopted midway between the author and the action, the first-person narrator recalling an episode that occurred many years previously, during his childhood. Moreover, not only is he reporting ironically his juvenile reactions to the series of extraordi-

nary events, but he also admits he was a mere bystander, never an
active participant, and that his imagination and memory may have
deceived him. Through the use of these devices, the author
achieves a remarkable degree of detachment, casts doubt on the
narrator's reliability, and thus charges his tale with an extraordinar-
ily heavy dose of irony.

Verbal irony in "Paseo" stems principally from the mature narrator's tongue-in-cheek recollections of his childlike reactions to the
adult members of his family. Thus, the boy, his aunt, and her three
brothers become victims of irony, all of them confidently unaware of
the dangers lurking beneath the surface and around the edges of
their perfectly ordered universe. For the narrator the living symbol
of this rigid perfection and security is his Aunt Mathilda who anticipates a comfortable heaven "identical to our house" (p. 311) and
envisions a hell that does not exist for them, naturally, but rather for
"those anonymous seamen who caused the damages that, when the
cases were concluded, filled the family coffers." (pp. 311–12) In
view of her strict set of values and behavior, Mathilda's ultimate fate
constitutes the story's most striking example of incongruity.

The child's marginal role and desire to enter "that circle of imprisoned affections" are frequently alluded to ironically. His aunt
turns down her brothers' beds each evening but not her nephew's
because he is not her brother. "And not to be 'one of my brothers'
seemed to her a misfortune of which many people were victims,
almost all in fact, including me, who after all was only the son of one
of them." (p. 311) Only during the ritualistic game of billards does
the isolated youngster achieve a limited sense of belonging when,
after each play, he is allowed to chalk his father's cue with the blue
cube. "With this minimal role that he [the boy's father] assigned to
me, he let me touch the circle that united him with the others,
without letting me take part in it more than tangentially." (p. 313)

Frequent reference is made in "Paseo" to the dark, magic world
of the port city which has no place in the characters' rationally
oriented lives but which, little by little, poses a terrible threat to
them. The dog enters the house mysteriously at night, and when
Mathilda begins to take her pet for long walks, her nephew suspects
that the two of them are partners in some nefarious scheme, shel-
tered by the mysterious nocturnal sounds of the city. The mongrel's
incongruous presence in the household and its devastating effect on
Mathilda's destiny constitute an eruption of the grotesque into the

family's orderly way of life and strike a blow at rationalism by demonstrating the absurdity of positing absolutes in a world buffeted by the blind forces of chaos. "Paseo" is a classic example of the irony of fate. Its subtle portrayal of the hidden realities of human existence unveils new areas of awareness and, at the same time, heightens aesthetic appreciation.

Three relatively unimportant tales, not included in *Cuentos,* also reveal marked traces of irony.[23]

III *Aesthetic Aspects*

The casual reader of Donoso's short fiction is likely to be impressed by its many characteristics of nineteenth and early twentieth-century realism: the presentation of Chilean customs, especially of the middle and upper-middle classes; the succinct, analytical style; the impeccably structured plots; and the traditional literary techniques. However, as critic Alexander Coleman has warned, to see nothing more than "a perfectly calculated kind of realistic literary practice" in the stories is "to hide their insidious and quite beautifully disguised thematics."[24]

Donoso is a masterful creator of dialogues, visual scenes, and moods, all of which lend vitality to his psychological portraits and enrich the texture of his fictional fabric. In most of the stories the reader's sensibilities are engaged by terse conversations and sensual descriptions that unmask the protagonists and set the stage for character or plot development. The first paragraph of "China," the story of the child who accompanies his mother to an exotic working-class district, depicts all the fascinating sights, sounds, smells, and movement certain to capture the youngster's imagination and thus determine the theme. "Paseo" owes its atmosphere of isolation, mystery, repressed sensuality, and rising tension to passages like the following:

The silence of the room was filled with the secret voice of each object: a grain of dirt trickling down between the wallpaper and the wall, the creaking of polished woods, the quivering of some loose crystal. Someone, in addition to ourselves, was where we were. A small white form came out of the darkness near the service door. The bitch crossed the vestibule, limping slowly in the direction of Aunt Mathilda, and without even looking at her, threw herself down at her feet. (pp. 316–17)

And Donoso also skillfully captures the suffocating drabness of boarding houses where three of his protagonists (Alberto Aldea of "Fiesta en grande," Santelices of "Santelices," and Sebastián Rengifo of "The Closed Door") grope for a sense of transcendence amidst ritualistic canasta games, domineering maternal figures, soap operas, and lingering kitchen odors.

The majority of Donoso's tales are linear in structure, with every detail aimed at a steadily rising climax and rapid ending. "The Güero," "Charleston," "Paseo," and "The Dane's Place" develop plots in circular form, beginning at the end and then chronologically retracing the entire course of events. Only three stories deviate from the above formula. An omniscient author introduces and concludes the mélange of present and past occurrences contained in "Dos cartas." The action of "Santelices," initially set in motion by the discovery of the protagonist's pictures, includes two flashbacks which relate happenings from the immediate and remote past before progressing with rhythmic repetition to the dramatic climax. And "Ana Maria," perhaps the most modern in its structure, displays a montage of spatially dislocated scenes that disrupt temporal progression but never erase the general impression of lineality.

The Chilean author's manipulation of the narrative point of view in his short fiction is, like his treatment of language and time, traditional and carefully executed. Of his fourteen most important stories, seven are told in the first person by the protagonist or a witness-narrator, six are related by a third-person narrator, and one, "Dos cartas," alternates between these two methods. In his stories told in the third person Donoso varies aesthetic distance (the appropriate distance between the reader and the fictional material) in order to control the reader's involvement and achieve maximum effect. Thus, the omniscient narrator's point of view is often replaced by that of one of the characters whose mind serves as a highly polished mirror to reflect the fictional world the author wishes to represent. When filtered through the consciousness of a so-called third-person reflector, this world is brought closer to the reader who tends to identify more readily with the character and share his dramatic situation. Two stories illustrating the use of the reflector technique are "Fiesta en grande," in which the timid office clerk Alberto Aldea is dominated by his mother, and "Santelices," the tale of the sadomasochistic boarding-house dweller who leaps to his death from his office window. The tragic lives of these protagonists achieve greater poignancy due to the fact that much of what happens to them is presented from their points of view.

One of Donoso's shortest, simplest, and yet most carefully executed stories is "Tocayos" (Namesakes), a sketch of a seventeen-year-old waitress named Juana who is seduced by her friend Juan the night before he leaves for a year's service in the army. This tale's spare, impersonal prose, stark realism, and emphasis on concrete detail, characterize the stylized slice-of-life fiction, reminiscent of Hemingway, that became a pervasive literary mode of expression in Chile during the 1950's. The omniscient author briefly describes Juan Acevedo, a young mechanic, and Señor Hernández, the owner of a modest café where the two men often pass the time drinking and playing dominoes. From the moment Juana is introduced on the second page, hers becomes the principal point of view, the only mind entered. Seen solely through her innocent eyes, the other two characters seem flat in comparison to the protagonist whose silent thoughts and mounting erotic tension form the story's warp and woof and lead to the logical climax. By exploring the girl's consciousness and narrowing his narrative perspective to her limited field of vision, the author captures the rigid set of values controlling her existence and heightens the story's impact on the reader. The following passages illustrate the dialectical interplay between Juana's physical surroundings and emotional undercurrents:

She confessed her impatience [to see Juan again] to Rosa who diagnosed her feelings as love. It was a marvelous discovery because it was her first love, just like in the movies. Rosa would often tell her about her experiences with men and Juana felt very envious, hoping for the day when she would be able to tell her friend not only that she was in love but that she had a "firm commitment." She understood the seriousness of the difference. And it was simply humiliating for Rosa to define her feelings before she herself knew what they were. But that wasn't surprising since Rosa was three years older and blonde. (p. 49)

But she kept looking at him: he had bought a brown suit secondhand. The coat fit him well but the trousers were too big . . . Nevertheless, he didn't look bad, especially when he wore his blue scarf around his neck. (p. 51)

He embraced her, kissing her on the mouth. She let him do it, feeling all his strength against her body. But she didn't move because she would not have known what to do. (p. 52)

. . . She soon went to sleep, thinking of the expression of Rosa's face the next day when she would tell her that at last she had "a firm commitment." (p. 53)

Virtually all of Donoso's short stories leave an impression of unity, a quality achieved not only through stylistic, technical, and structural devices, but also through the incorporation of recurring symbols, images, and rhythmic speech patterns which integrate language with plot, expand meaning, and lend texture and resonance to the material. Previously mentioned motifs conveying what the author cannot or does not wish to express conceptually include the old, dilapidated house in "Summertime"; the protagonist's pistol in "Fiesta en grande"; the fat man in "Charleston"; the door in "The Closed Door"; Ana María's hypnotic eyes in the story bearing her name; the white mongrel in "Paseo"; the title's allusion to the child narrator's imagination and innocence in "China"; the ubiquitous woman in a green raincoat in "A Lady"; and the blond protagonist in "The Güero."

Donoso occasionally begins and ends his tales with similar ideas or representations, a balancing device that circumscribes his fictional world and lends structural unity to his compositions. Thus, the protagonist of "A Lady" imagines the first and final scenes to be reproductions of others experienced at some time in the past; the aura of mystery and the massive library door muffling the sound of voices from within stand out both at the beginning and end of "Paseo"; and "The Dane's Place" focuses initially on the narrator's arrival at an outpost in southern Chile and, ultimately, on his departure from the same place.[25]

A sense of rhythm and tonality emerges in several stories as a result of repetitive phrasing which augments momentum or creates harmony or contrast. Both tension and greater cohesiveness characterize "Charleston" due to the recurring rhythms evoked by the dance (the Charleston) and the numerous references to the fear triggered by the fat man's agony. A similar situation occurs in "Paseo" with the steadily increasing tension between Mathilda's perfectly ordered household and the frequently mentioned mysterious forces emanating from the port city. This precarious balance is of course dealt a shattering blow by the denouement.

Repetition in "The 'Hombrecito,' " Donoso's only piece of short fiction with an overt social theme, produces less successful results. The protagonist of this story is a capable, young jack-of-all-trades whose unhappy private life and addiction to alcohol eventually become evident to the narrator's upper-class family. As his situation worsens, the workman's oft-reiterated phrase, "What do you people know about what happens to people like us?" is intended to intensify the reader's compassion and emphasize the dichotomy between the upper and lower classes in Chilean society. The repetition of this obvious social message, however, becomes tedious and excessively rhetorical, making "The 'Hombrecito' " one of Donoso's least interesting works.

Perhaps the best example of rhythm in Donoso's stories appears in "Santelices" where, through the use of Expressionistic techniques,[26] the momentum generated by the protagonist's madness is reflected in his hallucinations, growing hostility toward his landlady, and, ultimately, his suicidal leap. From the moment Santelices discovers the girl playing with her cat in a garden below his office window, the tempo of events begins to quicken. As the kittens grow and multiply, Santelices' encounters with Doña Berta become increasingly tense. Finally, after reducing his domineering landlady to tears, he retires and soon thereafter loses all contact with reality: ". . . the jungle was growing within him now, with its roars and flashes of heat, with its effusions of life and death." (p. 281) Imagining the girl to be in danger, he rushes to his office, and looks out the window.

> He stifled a shriek of horror: the patio was a viscous hotbed of beasts from which all the eyes—yellow, garnet, gold, green—were looking at him. . . . Where was the girl? . . . more and more tigers with flashing eyes jumped from the wall into the patio. Ocelots, hungry pumas were clawing the strips of darkness among the violet leaves. Ounces were killing lynxes. . . . Everything was cracking, roaring . . .
>
> Santelices was not afraid. . . . The branches were cleared away down below . . . there she was; yes, she was begging him to save her. . . . The night was filled with flashing eyes; above, in the sky, through the enormous branches which were stifling him, and down below, in the swarm of beasts that were devouring each other. . . . There was the girl waiting for him; perhaps she was moaning . . . he had to save her. . . . With a shriek he . . . made a ferocious leap in order to reach her. (pp. 282–84)

From the aesthetic point of view Donoso's most perfect short story is "Paseo." Although this tale alludes to modern man's existential crisis, it is above all a work of art in the Henry James tradition, the creation of an intense illusion, a sealed-off, self-contained entity, rather than an imitation of reality. Divided into four parts,[27] "Paseo" creates an initial air of isolation, suspense, and fear by foreshadowing a mysterious, climactic event. "Now I think that perhaps they [Mathilda's three brothers] were right in wanting to blot out everything. For why should one live with the terror of having to acknowledge that the streets of a city can swallow up a human being, leaving him without life and without death, suspended as it were, in a dimension more dangerous than any dimension with a name?" (p. 308) The subsequent alternation between the summary-narration of the household's routine and the intense scenes[28] introducing elements of animal vitality and irrational change comes to an abrupt end with Mathilda's disappearance and a return to the original state of affairs. "Life continued in the house just as if Aunt Mathilda were still living there." (p. 324)

Like much of James' work, "Paseo" shuns direct reference to everyday reality or abstract ideology and concentrates on tone, composition, and the subtle nuances of human relationships. Indeed, Mathilda and her brothers emerge as fictitious characters created within the circumscribed world of art rather than as real people drawn from life. The ironic contrast between the detached tone of the middle-aged narrator and his ingenuous childhood reactions to the strange occurrences he recalls underlies the tensions of opposites that breathe life into this tale: the lucidity of events and the ambiguity of cause; the protagonist's rational consciousness and her instinctual subconscious; and the household's rigid order and the eruption of chaos. The end result is a masterful and compelling synthesis of organic unity which depicts a kind of pure culture neurosis and jars the reader onto new levels of perception. In these respects "Paseo" provides an excellent introduction to much of Donoso's subsequent fiction.

CHAPTER 3

A Period of Transition
(1957–1966)

I   Coronation

PUBLISHED nine years apart, *Coronación (Coronation)*, 1957, and *Este domingo (This Sunday)*, 1966, have much in common but, at the same time, reveal fundamental differences that demonstrate Donoso's maturation as an artist and his growing awareness of the new literary trends throughout Latin America.[1] Because of their similarities and contrasts these two novels encompass a transitional phase in their author's total literary production and are thus treated within the same unit of this study.

Coronation depicts the lives of Misiá Elisa Grey de Abalos, a well-to-do, demented nonagenarian finishing out her existence in a rickety mansion, and her indolent, bachelor grandson Andrés, in his fifties, who has frittered away much of his life reading French history and collecting canes. The pleasant monotony of Andrés' hermetic world is disturbed when his long-dormant sexual instincts are aroused by Estela, a country girl brought in to care for the bedridden Misiá Elisa. Estela's affair with a youth named Mario from a nearby shantytown connects the two principal levels of society portrayed in the novel. The story climaxes and ends with Misiá Elisa's death, the madness of Andrés and the flight of Estela and her lover after their abortive attempt to carry off the household silver. Other important characters include Andrés' lifelong friend, Dr. Carlos Gros; Misiá Elisa's two servants, Rosario and Lourdes, who have devoted their entire adult lives to the Abalos family; Mario's impoverished half-brother René, an older man with criminal tendencies; and René's wife Dora.

One of the best Chilean novels published during the 1950's,

59

Coronation is, generally speaking, lineal in form, traditional in technique and naturalistic in the cause-and-effect delineation of its characters, most of whom are products of their environment. For example, the photographic description of Misiá Elisa's deteriorating house and garden in the book's initial pages provide an appropriate setting for the first appearance of the lethargic, middle-aged Andrés who in his youth studied law, not out of interest or enthusiasm for the legal profession, but because in his upper-class family it was considered the correct thing to do. Dora also has been molded by her milieu, the most obvious influences of which are a poor marriage and poverty. Formerly a pretty, happy-go-lucky factory worker, she is well on her way to becoming a shrewish, toothless hag. Social determinism is perhaps most evident, however, in the case of Mario whose mounting fear of entrapment climaxes with Estela's pregnancy and, subsequently, a poignant scene in which a moaning pregnant woman he encounters on a streetcar begs him to take her to the hospital.

No! No! He wasn't going to be trapped into this, not for anyone . . .
He rushed into the hospital, woke the dozing attendant and told him what had happened, and then ran away. It was Estela he was running from, for good this time; horror and repugnance had completely blotted out the tenderness of an hour before. It was Estela's long-drawn-out cries that pierced his ears as he ran, and again at home, as he tossed and turned in bed, unable to shut out the groans that stabbed the silence of the night, or to find sleep until dawn.[2]

Coronation also contains many of the short stories' literary elements and thematic obsessions such as recurring symbols, false rituals, and rigid daily routines, all of which tend to take possession of the characters and dominate their lives. These obsessions are related to the most significant facets of Freudian psychology, including 1) the importance of early childhood in determining the adult character, 2) the dark, unconscious layer of the mind, and 3) the centrality of sexual issues in human existence. Freud viewed both the individual and society as more irrational than rational, the mind constituting a kind of hell from which impulses erupt and threaten civilization. He also exposed the sham of bourgeois sexual mores that he believed produced neuroses through the repression of instincts and sexual pleasure. Freudian psychoanalysis sought a better understanding of man by unmasking the original self and making the unconscious conscious.

The most obvious examples of Freudian repression in *Coronation* are found in Misiá Elisa and Andrés, both of whom have been molded by bourgeois puritanism. Misiá Elisa in particular becomes obsessed with sexuality which, restrained and relegated to the unconscious for most of her life, undermines the rational processes and bursts forth in her old age in the form of obscenities, usually evoked by symbolic images. For example, the pink shawl Andrés brings her as a birthday gift suggests lasciviousness, a trait she attributes to Estela and Andrés. ("Come on, girl. Let's see you try on this pretty pink shawl he's brought you. He wouldn't have chosen a shawl like that for me. . . .it isn't the sort of thing you give a lady with the virtue of a saint and royal blood in her veins. It's a whore's shawl, do you hear? Go on, you slut, try it on! . . .Indian whore! You've been showing him your filthy tricks in bed, haven't you?" p. 55)

On another occasion Misiá Elisa warns Estela about the danger of being seduced and having an illegitimate child because, although men swear eternal love, they "are all the same, all pigs." (p. 92) By way of contrast, she considers herself a saint (I was so good, so moral. . . . never once in all my married life did I let Ramón see me naked!" p. 117), and sees life as a cesspool from which religion offers the only refuge. Even her doctor's explanation for her madness is expressed in terms vaguely reminiscent of Freud. "Everything she has kept hidden all these years, out of fear or shame or insecurity, erupts into her life once the conscious censor is relaxed, and peoples it with these fantasmal presences. . . ."(p. 19)

The pink, moist palms of Estela's hands arouse Andrés' dormant sexual desires which, detected by his grandmother, are intensified when the old lady accuses him of having an affair with the girl. Several hours after this disconcerting scene, Andrés takes a nap and dreams of episodes involving his sexual awakening as a boy[3]—a conversation about prostitutes he overheard in the restroom at school, Father Damián's and Misiá Elisa's stern warnings against sin, his distorted visions of hell, and his false confession and First Communion. Andrés' dream also evokes his philosophical rejection of religion which occurred at the time he was studying law.

Calling upon rational arguments that were really only a mask for his childhood fears, he speedily demolished the religious faith through which his grandmother had caused him so much suffering . . .In the last analysis, everything was a big question mark. And the more he read the more shifting and treacherous became the ground beneath his feet. (p. 68)

This loss of faith leads to his recollection of a nightmare he experienced repeatedly as a young man.

He used to dream that he was rushing across a long, long bridge slung out over a void. But the bridge abruptly came to an end before reaching the opposite bank, leaving a space in which there was nothing at all, only emptiness. In his haste and anxiety to reach the other side, Andrés always fell off the end, screaming with terror as he found himself hurtling through the void. He would wake up sweating and terrified. There was nothing in either philosophy or science . . . which gave him the means of arriving, whole and conscious, on the other side. Everything ended in a zero, in another question, the question mark of death itself. (p. 69)

This nightmare dramatizes the existentialist concept of the absurd, i.e., finite man searching for reason and meaning in an infinite, meaningless universe and his terror of being confronted with the void of death.[4] Andrés' anguish over this inevitable fate generates strong feelings of solitude which are demonstrated by the following episode. One day while still a young man he finds himself walking through a crowded, lower-class district of the city when a little girl looks up from her game of hopscotch, calls him "four-eyes" and then resumes her play. It occurs to him a few seconds later that this child has already completely forgotten him and that throughout her life she will probably never think of him again. His feelings of loneliness evoke his previously mentioned nightmare, but in this moment of despair his instinct for survival elicits from him an ironic remark that temporarily relieves his anguish.

"Everything is the same as it would be in . . . in . . ." He tried to think of the most remote, exotic place on earth, "in Omsk, say, and all these people were Omskians." . . . But of course, this street and these people were exactly the same as they would be in Omsk! . . . He saw people and things stretching out their hands to each other across centuries and kilometers; there were no longer any differences to make them objects of terror: all Omskians, himself included, were living a common destiny. They were all blind . . . but equally and universally blind amidst the chaos, a chaos that might be changed to order if one simply accepted the impossibility of arriving at the truth and stopped tormenting oneself with responsibilities and questions to which there were no answers. Compromises did not exist. There was only matter, caught up in the phenomenon of life, awaiting extinction. That was all. . . . to rebel, try . . . and cross the confines of the present, all this was stupid, pretentious, and puerile. And responsibilities and compromises were still more so. The only reasonable attitude was one of silent, passive acceptance. (pp. 72–73)

Andrés' attempt to reduce his feelings of solitude and anxiety by sharing them with others illustrates Sartre's contention that man can escape alienation through identification with one of two groups: 1) those who act, whom the French philosopher calls the "We-subject," and 2) those who remain passive, whom he calls the "Us-object."[5] Andrés chooses the latter, resigning himself to his fate. The distant Russian city of Omsk, then, embodies the isolation, meaninglessness, and nothingness which afflict all human beings and serve to justify Andrés' inability to act.

It freed him from the necessity of making any compromises with life. The little girl was playing hopscotch. . . . A man smoking on a street corner while a woman laughed. He, Andrés Abalos, was merely one among them, a solitary wanderer at any point, any moment in the universe. (p. 74)

This attitude, which has governed Andrés' conduct for more than two decades, changes abruptly as a result of Estela's disturbing presence, the terrifying knowledge of his grandmother's approaching death, and the realization that, unlike his friend Carlos Gros, he has never really lived. He attempts in vain to break out of his stagnant routine by purchasing an additional cane for the collection he has always limited to ten, but his failure in this enterprise and his discovery that Estela is in love with Mario only intensify his horror of encroaching nothingness, a subject he debates with Carlos Gros. A foil for Andrés' extreme pessimism, Gros extols love, science, free will and religion, all of which Andrés vehemently rejects:

Don't you realize that everything is a mess, an injustice, a mad trick played on us by the Cosmos? If there is a God who watches over man's destiny, he must be a mad God. What could be more absurd than giving men the faculties to perceive the chaos and terror around them, and not giving them anything to conquer them with? No, Carlos, don't lie to yourself—the only truth is madness because the mad are the only ones who see that everything is chaos, and that explaining, clarifying, reasoning are futile. Being helpless, they realize that the only way to reach the truth is to let themselves be swallowed up by the greater madness. To sane men, like ourselves, all that remains is the terror . . . (p. 186)

These words foreshadow the protagonist's ultimate surrender to madness which occurs immediately after Estela repulses his advances and runs away with Mario. Unable to face the emptiness of his remaining years ("He was just a thing, matter poised before its return to the void . . ." p. 253), Andrés severs all ties with reality, rejecting even his previously held concept of death and nothingness: "Death was just a fable, a bogeyman to frighten naughty children with, and his life would go on forever." (p. 258) His denial of his absurd fate constitutes an escape from freedom and responsibility[6] that typifies Donoso's characters but contrasts sharply with the revolt through action of the absurd heroes of existential literature.

Although serious philosophical, psychological, and social themes play a major role in the Chilean author's first novel, a measure of balance is achieved through occasional irony and numerous aesthetic elements. The incongruity of a 94-year-old prude spewing forth obscenities one moment and expressing religious fervor the next, though not without pathos, can be hilarious, and her incessant chatter alternating between pure madness and uncanny intuition makes up some of the book's most memorable passages.

Andrés also provides a rich source of irony, especially the episodes relating his adolescent ignorance and curiosity about religion and sex. The characters involved in these passages are seen through a child's innocent eyes, thus increasing the distance between the narrator and his subject matter and enhancing the possibilities for situational irony. Andrés recalls Father Damián's booming voice that could be heard throughout most of the school ("*Hell* was the word he used most, and when he said it his face and eyes went red and his mouth looked like a black hole." p. 60), and he suspected that there was a connection between the underworld and the washroom because the latter was a dirty place and the only part of the building where Father Damián's voice did not penetrate. On one occasion when Andrés was in the washroom he overheard two older boys refer to servants as whores, and upon returning home he set off a flurry of indignation by asking Lourdes, his grandmother's housekeeper, if she was one. Misiá Elisa's stern but vague admonitions regarding sexual matters served to confuse him even more. ("There were things she herself did not understand at all, and sincerely hoped she never would." p. 63) Meanwhile he began to hate school because the two students whose conversation he had overheard were forcing him to look at pornographic pictures. He also had sexual nightmares about a pink chair in his grandmother's room which he somehow connected with the short, chubby Lourdes. All these problems together with his antipathy for Father Damián prevented him from confessing his transgressions before his First Communion and convinced him he had received the Host in mortal sin. "It was not, as they had assured him it would be, 'the happiest day of his life.' " (p. 65)

As indicated previously in the discussion of the short stories, Donoso frequently abandons the traditional technique of total authorial omniscience by penetrating the minds of his characters and interpreting their thoughts indirectly in third-person narration. This procedure, which was utilized extensively by Henry James, offers a plurality of perspectives and augments plausibility and dramatic intensity by allowing the reader to identify more directly with one or more viewpoint characters or third-person reflectors. The following passage begins and ends with the author's interpretation of Andrés' sentiments about death and, although it consists entirely of the protagonist's intimate, unspoken thoughts, the long central portion conveys information about his friend Carlos Gros. Thus Andrés emerges as a third-person reflector whose personal feelings heighten the contrast between himself and Carlos.

Andrés suddenly thought about his grandmother dying, and snatched, horrified, at the notion that she must never die, never . . . because if she died he would cease to live too, assuming he ever had lived. How he envied Carlos what he had always regarded as his defects ! There was a lot to be said against him. But it no longer seemed to matter that his schoolgirl gushing about love made him appear ridiculous; though certainly, with his short, plump figure, stubby fingers, and face like softened red Plasticine, it was both ludicrous and unaesthetic to imagine him making love. Moreover, he was ambitious and had let his youthful scientific passion be corrupted into a desire to make money and achieve a reputation. He was base, promiscuous, even lachrymose in his love affairs. . . . But he could not deny that Carlos always threw himself wholeheartedly into everything . . . He had given his instincts free rein, he had respected them, he had believed. When he was on his deathbed, he would have the consolation of knowing he had tasted a good portion of human experience with all the intensity he was capable of. And he, Andrés ? He saw himself, suddenly, on his deathbed, and he was seized by a wild desire to run away, screaming with terror, go back fifty years and live through it all again, quite differently. (p. 86)

Coronation, like the short stories, is replete with recurring symbols and images that expand meaning and, at the same time, enrich the literary fabric with unifying patterns. Misiá Elisa's deteriorating mansion with its "profusion of little turrets, unnecessary gables, terraces and balconies that did not open out of any room" (p. 189) represents a decadent, outmoded way of life and, for Andrés, a kind of lost paradise to which he is ultimately drawn. The palms of Estela's hands and Misiá Elisa's shawl become sexual obsessions that intensify Andrés' disturbed state of mind and accelerate the plot's tempo. Another recurring image is that of a stuffed rabbit with green spots which Dora has proudly created to sell for desperately needed cash. It first appears in her home during a quarrel between herself and Mario, then in Misiá Elisa's kitchen where for Andrés it becomes an object of ridicule, and finally, at the end of the book, in the deranged Andrés' surrealistic account of his grandmother's coronation. A kind of evolving symbol, this toy animal serves to link episodes and reflect contrasting mental states and attitudes. Also symbolic is Dora's toothless mouth, a grotesque remnant of her youthful beauty and the mark of exploitation left on her by her worthless, domineering husband.

Andrés' collection of ten canes occupies a focal point in the novel, representing the rigid limits he has imposed on his sterile, routine existence in order to strengthen his hold on life and fend off the threat of chaos. His efforts to increase the number of canes in his collection take him to the home of an antique dealer whose wife's pink shawl and naked palms evoke from his subconscious the same disturbing images he has suppressed since the day of his grandmother's birthday party. He leaves the antique shop abruptly and, while walking through the evening mist, becomes fully aware of his desire for Estela whose affection, if not love, he resolves to win. However, as he approaches his grandmother's house, the sight of the girl talking with her lover under a streetlight makes him aware of the absurdity of his situation and initiates his gradual retreat from reality into madness.

Donoso's interest in art is evident in numerous parts of *Coronation*. For example, the final portion of Chapter 9 and the initial lines of Chapter 10 depict two love scenes which, linked back to back, resemble a diptych. The two passages are connected by the flight of a bird that circles "for a long while high over the recumbent pair [René and Dora], keeping watch in the perfectly blue lookout post of the air" (p. 111) and then, in the ensuing chapter, flies off toward the mountains, eventually gliding over a younger couple (Mario and Estela), "locked together in the bushes on a slope that faced the setting sun." (p. 111) In addition to a kind of double painting, these two scenes constitute a montage of contrasts—experience, innocence, maturity, youth—which accentuate each other and contribute to the novel's aesthetic balance.

One of the artistic movements that has most fascinated Donoso is Art Nouveau, an ornamental style that flourished in Europe and America between 1890 and 1910. Several passages portraying Misiá Elisa suggest an influence of this school which is characterized by opulence of detail, voluptuous curves, decorative floral borders' bold massing of dark and light patches, and two-dimensional patterns on flat surfaces. While still an attractive, middle-aged woman, Misiá Elisa is depicted in elegant attire as she is about to be photographed by her husband.

Finally the boy [Andrés] made his way to the veranda where his grandmother was waiting, rocking herself to and fro in her Viennese bentwood chair in the midst of a veritable jungle of ferns, dwarf palms, begonias, and great pots planted with thickets of bamboo. When she saw her grandson coming, she smiled and put up her parasol . . . "Are we ready, then? Shall we go?"

. . . .

Grandfather stood waiting for them beside the camera, fanning himself with his straw boater. His wife took her seat on the stone bench—carved to look like twisted tree trunks—and the full skirt of her lilac dress billowed out around her as she bent forward from the waist, with both hands resting on the handle of her parasol. (pp. 14–15)

The pictorial depictions of Misiá Elisa's "coronation" and death display the bold use of lighting effects, the lack of depth perception, and the vivid, rococo delicacy of bows, streamers, and shimmering spangles that typify Art Nouveau paintings. Her "unearthly" look in an "illuminated niche" and her imagined ascent amidst the stars, moreover, suggest a portrait of the Virgin Mary's ascent heavenward.

. . . while the old lady slept on, they [her two servants] rushed about making the room look suitable for a coronation. They ranged the vases of flowers around Misiá Elisa and scattered some white petals at her feet. Then Lourdes concealed some lamps among the flowers so that they lit up Misiá Elisa's face. Rosario tied bows and streamers to her walking stick . . . The lighting made Misiá Elisa look unearthly, isolating her in an il-luminated niche of flowers in the midst of the darkened room. (p. 238)

There was barely a flicker of life left in the old woman now, and only the dimmest spark of consciousness. However, she could see the stars through the rain-streaked windows, and having lost the power to distinguish be-tween near and far and seeing nothing but sparkling lights all the way up from the showers of spangles on the floor to the brilliants on her coronation gown, she thought that these were stars too and that she was surrounded by them. Then she supposed that she must already be dead and that she was ascending very gently through the firmament straight to heaven. (p. 262)

Donoso's characters often reveal contrasts and parallels which create tension, balance, and compositional unity. Andrés and Mario, for example, offer striking differences in age, appearance, temper-ament, and social standing, but a surprising number of existential similarities determine their destinies. Both belong to a club which plays a role in molding their sense of values and obliges them to conform to the norms of their class. Thus, Mario must wear the figurative mask of a Don Juan-sportsman, while Andrés feels com-pelled to play the role of the dignified, conservative, never-too-ec-centric intellectual. The two also share a strong attraction to Estela who represents an element of danger for each of them. However, whereas the older man is profoundly disturbed by the girl's physical appearance and his grandmother's wild accusations of their affair, Mario is afraid of being trapped into marriage, especially after Es-tela becomes pregnant.

Both Andrés and Mario suffer from other obsessive fears, the former from old age and death, intensified by his contacts with Misiá Elisa, and the latter from a dreaded criminal destiny similar to that of his brother, René. In both cases these fears generate surrealistic nightmares that express deep-seated anxieties in symbolic images, Andrés' previously mentioned fall from a truncated bridge into a chasm, and Mario's punishment upon being dragged by a man re-sembling René "toward something terrifying, through whole bat-talions of policemen . . . who swarmed and multiplied like ants, covering everything in sight in his dreams." (p. 159)

The Omsk episode conveying Andrés' unconscious efforts to suppress his solitude and despair is echoed by an incident involving Mario during his search for René in Valparaíso. Wandering along the quay he catches sight of the word "Oslo" written on the prow of a ship which dock workers are loading with sacks of rice. Mario begins to think of the distant city as a means of escape. "Oslo . . . Perhaps it was a mirage conjured from this transparent day to make him regret that he was here at all and forget René and the destiny marked out for him." (p. 200) And later that night while sitting in a bar filled with sailors he feels a "sudden urgent longing to become one of them, sign on with some boat which would take him a long way from this crushed existence of his. Oslo? Was there really a place with a name like a furry toy? Go away forever." (p. 201)

Both Andrés and Mario experience a series of crises that propel them along parallel trajectories toward their respective fates. More Freudian by nature, Andrés' crises include his early encounters with Estela and his grandmother's intuitive suggestions of his sexual attraction for the girl; his explosive reaction to the antique dealer's wife, Tenchita, who makes him fully aware of his desire for Estela; and Estela's ultimate rejection of him, which precipitates his flight into madness. Mario's traumatic experiences, brought about by social deterministic forces, are the loss of his job and impoverishment, Estela's pregnancy, his brother's nefarious influences, and the climactic episode with the pregnant woman on the streetcar.

Closely related to these events affecting the lives of both characters is the hint of fused identities destined to become a major theme in *The Obscene Bird of Night* and *Sacred Families*. Andrés at times experiences an intuitive fear of both his grandmother and her house, preferring his orderly life in an apartment by himself. On one occasion he recalls that the last time he spent the night in the room above Misiá Elisa's, he was distracted from his reading by the muffled sound of her voice, a purring, deranged monologue which oozed into his room and created a frightening air of madness.

Andrés got no sleep at all that night. He was sweating all over, on his bald head and on his neck and even on his hands, which were usually dry-skinned. . . . The reality of his grandmother's insanity had been driven deep into his mind, expelling any other thoughts or feelings and throwing him completely off balance.

The memory of that night armored him against any temptation to repeat the experience. He was much better off as he was, in his own apartment, which held no mysteries and was both exceedingly comfortable and very much his own, the perfect setting for his self-contained bachelor existence, with its strict routine. Whereas this house, where the very woodwork was permeated with the sick woman's voice, represented a serious threat to Andrés' mental equilibrium. (pp. 43–44)

And at the end of the novel when Andrés returns to his grand-mother's home and loses touch with reality, he succumbs to the pervasive influence of the old lady whose madness has gradually undermined his rational processes and become an integral part of his own behavior.[7]

Mario's relationship with René resembles that of Andrés with Misiá Elisa. Fearful from the beginning of his brother's criminal nature, the youth detects an ever-tightening ring of danger from which he cannot extricate himself. His apprehensions reach a peak when he receives René's letter telling him to come to Valparaíso and bring money.

René had finally stretched out a hand to get him. And the frightening pain that had often made him fight people who called his brother a thief, the mysterious terror that made him glance behind him in dark streets, all the suspicions and anxieties that had haunted his life from afar were suddenly made real by this letter: he would have to go and find René and join him. (p. 161)

The subsequent episode in Valparaíso, the family's increasingly desperate financial straits and René's manipulative tactics eventually wear down Mario's resistance and induce him to participate in the theft of Misiá Elisa's silver.

The parallels between the lives of Andrés and Mario not only lend aesthetic cohesiveness to the novel but also demonstrate the irra-tional forces operating on two widely separated social levels. The tensions produced by these forces and by the injustices of a divided society leave the reader with little optimism for the future. Only the basically healthy instincts of the impoverished Mario and Estela, who escape into the night under "the gift of a cloudless sky" (p. 261), suggest a possible though dubious regeneration.

Despite its artistically inspired structure, philosophical depth and psychological probings, Donoso's first novel is not without serious defects. Andrés' dreams and conversations with Carlos Gros, though by no means devoid of interest, abound in rhetoric, leading the reader to view these two characters at times as abstract creations embodying preconceived philosophical concepts. Andrés' nightmarish confrontation with the existential void is too obviously an illustration of atheistic existentialism and Carlos too perfect a foil for the protagonist's foibles and obsessions. In spite of the book's stress on the irrational, Andrés' dream sequence and flight into madness are depicted in an objective, rational style similar to that of the more realistic episodes. Perhaps for these reasons the novel lacks the subtle integration of form and content and the vital tension between internal and external realities that characterize the author's subsequent works.

The ending of *Coronation* has been called absurd and melodramatic,[8] an assessment that has some validity. Nevertheless, although the plethora of climactic events on the final pages does raise questions concerning the story's verisimilitude, most facets of the denouement—the attempted robbery, Andrés' madness and Misiá Elisa's death—are logically and meticulously prepared beforehand. In fact, the reader's overall impression may well be that of the triumph of pattern and symmetry to the detriment of emotion and life. Still, Misiá Elisa emerges as one of Donoso's most successful creations. Her fluctuating moods constitute a rich source of irony, and the scenes depicting her "coronation"—by her drunken, aged servants, singing, dancing, and quarreling over a feather boa—and her demise are an imaginative mélange of humor, pathos, beauty, and the grotesque.

II This Sunday

In spite of its contemporary themes such as alienation and existential anguish, *Coronation* is fundamentally a traditional work, following stylistic and structural patterns similar to those discussed in the short stories and leaning heavily on psychological and social determinism for the development of its characters. As one might expect, during the long period between the publication of his first two novels (1957–1966), Donoso's literary orientation and aesthetic values changed noticeably. In fact, *Este domingo (This Sunday)*, 1966, indicates a new phase in the author's career characterized by a tendency to explore in greater depth the unconscious realm of his protagonists and the skillful integration of form and content. The end result is a fictional creation of greater intensity and artistic merit.[9]

The principal figures of *This Sunday* are Don Alvaro Vives and his wife Doña Chepa, a wealthy, middle-aged couple living in their large family home; Violeta, now retired but formerly a servant in the Vives household and Don Alvaro's mistress; and a psychopathic young man named Maya, of lower class origin, who has served more than nine years in prison on a murder conviction. In her role as a volunteer welfare worker, Chepa becomes involved with Maya, uses her family's influence to obtain his parole, and arranges to have him live in Violeta's home. The story ends with the murder of Violeta by Maya, the latter's voluntary return to prison, and the subsequent deaths of Don Alvaro and Doña Chepa. Other characters include the Vives' five grandchildren, one of whom narrates part of the book; Marujita Bueras, a peddler woman Maya meets while he is in prison; and Violeta's illegitimate daughter Mirella and son-in-law Fausto.

Much critical attention has been given to the similarities between *Coronation* and *This Sunday*. Both novels depict a rigidly stratified society consisting principally of a rich, decadent, domineering minority and an impoverished lower class; in both books a grandmother and her mansion play important symbolic roles; upper-class characters in both works become emotionally involved with members of the lower social strata; and the false-family theme is common to both novels as are several of the author's psychological and philosophical obsessions. The principal difference between *This Sunday* and its predecessor are due, above all, to the more recent book's adroit manipulation of innovative techniques and more subtle thematic development. Whereas in *Coronation* the omniscient author summarizes events, describes people and places photographically, and sharpens the narrative perspective by utilizing the characters as third-person reflectors, *This Sunday* achieves a contrapuntal effect by alternating between an ironically naive first-person narrator-participant and an occasional omniscient author. Most important in the second novel, however, is the successful use of the stream of consciousness, Donoso's first attempt to incorporate this technique into his work. As a result of these procedures, the lineal treatment of time in *Coronation* has been replaced in *This Sunday* by a more fluid temporal structure reflecting the literary and philosophical theories of Marcel Proust and Henry Bergson, which are discussed below. Finally, the Freudian and Sartrean concepts that stood out somewhat obtrusively in *Coronation* have become an integral part of the second novel's fictional world.

Don Alvaro's relations with Violeta are an interesting case in point. The passage describing the beginning of their affair is presented through Don Alvaro's stream of consciousness in the form of a flashback unleashed by the smell of the *empanadas*[10] for which he has gone to Violeta's house on Sunday morning. His recollection of the incident in question brings to mind the famous initial episode of Proust's *Remembrance of Things Past,* in which the taste of a *madeleine* (sponge cake) dipped in tea reminds the narrator of a similar taste he experienced many years previously, thus enabling him to recapture a whole segment of his long-forgotten past.[11]

In an instant the entire car is filled with the festive odor of hot *empanadas* . . . from all the Sundays of his life . . . It's Sunday. A bell rings in the neighborhood church. . . . This warm, golden smell . . . this smell of Sunday morning but not too early when the servants are busy in the house . . . one cleaning the living room . . . one humming in the kitchen while opening the oven to see how the *empanadas* are . . .[12]

Thus, through free association[13] Alvaro first remembers the Sunday mornings of his youth and then one specific Sunday during a summer vacation when the rest of his family had gone to the country, leaving him to study for a mathematics exam, with Violeta the only other occupant of the house. The sensuous style of the passage is enhanced by Freudian images which recur in a variety of patterns, suggesting the rhythmic acceleration of the young man's desire during the minutes before he and Violeta make love.

The two curtains flutter slightly, look for and then avoid each other, silhouettes that separate and brush each other and caress each other, suspended in the heat. (p. 43)
What happens in that dark embrace, in that heat like the curtains' silhouette, two bodies scarcely touching, dancing in the air?
. . . .
He stayed frozen in the middle of his room, nude, and the two bodies massaging each other, rubbing against each other in the window—he didn't breathe: outside the door, she too wasn't breathing, and above the storm of blood in his ears, he hears, he thinks he hears the delicate friction of her skin inside her clean clothing
. . . .

A bath . . . one floats in that greenish water like an enormous body enveloping him, brushing him like the two curtains. . . . (pp. 47–48)

Throughout his years in law school Alvaro visits Violeta in her
room after his dates with "good girls" who, in his words, are "only
meant for marrying . . . delicate as butterflies . . . not strong like
you, you that I can squeeze this way, you who aren't sacred because
you're a servant girl and can't expect anything from me the way that
they expect . . ." (p. 56) While making love to Violeta he tries to
"conjure up out of that warm, plump body the fineness of Pola's
arms, Alicia's long neck and small head, Sofia's young and barely
protruding breasts . . ." (p. 57) He admits to Violeta that university
girls and prostitutes frighten him, the former because they are ugly
and pretentious and the latter because they are dirty, but "you don't
frighten me, you're clean." (p. 56)

Thus, Alvaro emerges as a weak young man whose social position
enables him to exploit others without having to assume responsibilities. For him Violeta represents a minimum of effort and risk, a
situation which deprives her of an authentic life of her own and, in a
sense, anticipates her tragic end. In existentialist terms theirs is a
subject-object relationship, but without the usual conflict Sartre has
ascribed to most human associations.[14] Both Alvaro and Violeta are
examples of what Sartre calls bad faith; he because he destroys her
freedom and she because she escapes from the responsibility of a
free individual by accepting her role as an object.

Alvaro's attraction to girls of his own class is based more on social
convention than on love as, for example, in the case of Pola:

he loved her because she was beautiful and elegant and spoke his language
and the language of his family, and had his values and the values of his
family. Then his desire to have her for himself would scourge him: she was a
virgin and a decent girl and her parents had known his parents all their
lives . . . (p. 60)

His feelings for Chepa are similar to those he felt for Pola:

That hair like a black helmet. That chalk skin. Those architectural features. . . . The prettiest. The richest. The best in every way. . . . He
doesn't love her. But he's going to love her. He's sure of that because she
has everything he needs to love her, and she represents the best, the
pinnacle of his world. (p. 62)

Their wedding night is almost a disaster for Alvaro.

He caresses her admiringly, terrified in the face of so much perfection, but inert . . . He had to do something . . . to run away forever and hide his impotency and his terror beneath the earth, to flee . . . where no one would look for him: to Violeta's room . . . And closing his eyes . . . and sure of himself, he made love to Violeta in the ignorant flesh of Chepa. (pp. 68–69)

Now in their fifties, Alvaro and Chepa have ceased to live together as man and wife, both having donned "masks" as a means of protection or escape from their unsatisfactory realities. Alvaro's incapacity for love and his narcissistic withdrawal into himself are made increasingly evident by several incidents.[15] Referred to ironically as "the Doll" by his five grandchildren, he greets them briefly every Saturday in his study where he plays "interminable games of chess with a ghostly adversary." (p. 9) Although his deafness makes conversation difficult, the children also notice he does not seem to focus his eyes on them because

he was scrutinizing his own reflection in the glass doors of the bookcases, unnecessarily straightening the knot in his tie, passing his hand over the carefully combed hair that seemed to be painted on his head, as if in those glass doors he might find a perfect image of himself projected on the rich twilight of the bindings. He did not hear our answers partly because of his deafness, but more because he was not concerned enough to listen. (pp. 10–11)

The child narrator also wonders if his grandfather's ridiculous appearance might have been a calculated form of protection, "one more method of freeing himself from the commitment an individual relationship with us would have implied." (p. 11)

Chepa's basic insecurity and lack of love emerge from her unspoken interior monologues,[16] several of which take place in the prison where Maya is being held. In the first of these she is in the infirmary visiting the convict and alternately pondering her relations with her own family and the poor people she helps.

I know they, my daughters and my sons-in-law, whisper that I'm silly, that I don't understand them, that I'm superficial. But what else can I do? I can hold my own with poverty. And with filth. They're within my reach because

I'm only an ignorant woman: my governess didn't teach me anything except to read and write and do sums . . . . But I give *them* something that I know, when I teach them that they mustn't go on living in the filth, when I paper their rooms with newspaper . . . so let me help them . . . because I don't understand politics or history. (p. 96)

Another monologue which occurs in the warden's office conveys her conviction that Alvaro has reduced her to a meaningless object with no more significance than the drab, impersonal furnishings of a government bureau.

Páez [the warden] left Chepa alone in his office . . . A single bulb was hanging from a wire in the middle of the ceiling. Broken-down leather furniture. Calendars with nudes. A day-old rose in a vase . . . And the Underwood typewriters, funereal, enormous. Things. Objects that don't mean anything . . . Switch off as she does when Alvaro speaks, as she learned to after the first month of marriage when she became aware that he was not holding her in his arms when they were making love, but anyone, that for him . . . she was interchangeable. I am not me. I don't exist. (p. 114)

A recurrent image used in reference to Chepa, to underscore her sadomasochistic tendencies, is that of "a littered bitch . . . with hungry whelps stuck to her, sucking on her teats, never happy unless she can feel mouths that are thirsty for help, comfort, care, compassion, fastened to her breasts." (p. 22) This compulsion to give of herself also emerges from a conversation with her friend Fanny in which she attempts to justify her neglect of her family in order to secure Maya's release. "I feel so guilty for never having been a good wife to Alvaro or a good mother to the girls. You know they've never interested me. . . . No, don't think I'm a monster, but they stopped needing me so soon . . ." (p. 104)

It would seem, then, that Chepa's welfare activities represent a means of escape from her feelings of inferiority and aloneness, an escape brought about through her associations with people even more insecure than she is herself. However, her philanthropy is in reality a mask for her domineering nature which stifles love and other forms of normal human relationships.[17] These facets of her character become especially evident through her interior monologues which also shed light on her complex relations with Maya. For example, while expecting momentarily the news of the

young man's release from prison, she recalls her many conversations
with him on visitors' days, their mother-son attachment for each
other and her fears of losing him when he is set free.

She feels that tremor of pleasure, as though Maya were her baby and she
was giving him her breast bursting with milk . . . and he was sucking more
and more, as though from that mother who told a neighbor to take care of
the little boy for a couple of days while she and the miner she was living
with went to do some errands in another town, and she got on the bus, and
the barefoot boy . . . watches how the bus goes off in a cloud of
dust. . . . She didn't come back . . . And . . . Maya told her [Chepa] that
each time she went off through the patio [of the prison] it was like that time
with the cloud of dust, and he was afraid that she might forget him and
never come back again.
. . . .
    But when he gets out? What will I be to him when he gets out? He needs
me now. I'm the center of his life. But afterwards? Will he be like the girls
who left me, and like my grandchildren who might soon begin to leave me,
and like Alvaro who never . . .? I don't want him to get out. (pp. 111–12)

After Maya is granted parole Chepa helps him set up a leather
goods shop which thrives at first but eventually fails because of his
heavy losses at the horse races. Meanwhile, Chepa's vigilance over
his activities restricts his freedom, arouses his fierce resentment and
sparks his decision to go away. When Chepa learns on Sunday
morning that Maya has returned after a long absence, she goes to
Violeta's home to look for him and finds out not only that he and
Violeta have been lovers but that the previous evening he came to
her door in a drunken state demanding money. Violeta's description
of the incident reveals how Maya's deranged mind confused her
with Chepa while the latter's intervening interior monologue exposes her more-than-maternal feelings for Maya.

"And then, ma'am, then he really got furious, and he said all women were
the same as you—as that Chepa, he said. Damn her . . . she's such a saint,
every time she forgives me for something I want to do more and more bad
things . . . And he said I was just like you."
    Like me, but more enviable, Violeta, you who don't understand, you who
don't know, you who let yourself get carried away while I look on from the
periphery without confessing anything, I envy your bruises. Maya comes to
see you at night while I dry up waiting beside the telephone.
    ". . . just like you, that we both wanted to eat him, to swallow him, to

control him, to break him down, and that he wasn't going to let us, and then he began to hit me, Misiá Chepa. Look how that rat left me . . ." (pp. 143–144)

Violeta also admits to Chepa that she had an affair with Alvaro before his marriage, a revelation that precipitates the novel's most dramatic episode. Casting off her mask of altruism, Chepa sets out at once for the shantytown in search of Maya. "I want to go and look for him, light and free now, lashed by all kinds of winds . . . Not save him. Nothing but look for him. How easy it is to throw out a lie." (p. 153) Prior to this time she has entered only the outer edges of the sprawling slums by daylight, but on this occasion her intense desire to find the ex-prisoner takes her deep into the maze of alleys at twilight. She becomes disoriented almost immediately but somehow manages to locate Marujita Bueras, Maya's mistress, whose words only inflame her passions.

You know, he's afraid of you. Sometimes . . . he would talk about how good you'd been to him. . . . And other times . . . he says you're going to come and look for him to put him back to work again and go on spying on him. And sometimes . . . he says . . . you're hot for him. . . . and he cries because he misses you . . .
. . . .
because even though he talks bad of you he loves you. (p. 157)

As she frantically attempts to find her way out of the shantytown, Chepa experiences a surrealistic nightmare. Millions of eyes seem to be staring at her from out of the darkness, and the urchins following her, one of whom resembles a dwarf or an old woman, steadily increase in number. In a kind of masochistic delirium she envisions herself being devoured by the voracious poor.

They want something. To take things from her. That feeling she sometimes gets with the poor people of her shantytown: . . . they want to devour her, to take pieces of her flesh to feed themselves on, and sometimes, in her dreams, she feels that she has thousands of teats and all the thousands of inhabitants of her shantytown . . . are fastened to those teats, sucking them and soon they are no longer sucking but biting them, at first like someone playing a game and she feels pleasure and asks them to bite gently . . . but later they become enthusiastic and bite harder and harder and they draw blood . . . and she cries even more . . . but it's wonderful because they are feeding from her flesh and they grow fat and healthy from her and she wants to give herself to them even though they kill her with pain, no, don't kill her, the only thing she begs of them is that they leave her a tiny spark of life so she can be aware that she is feeding them. . . . (pp. 161–62)

When she enters the slum, Chepa is wearing, as she often did, a fur piece consisting of four martens. This unusual garment, which she admits has been long out of style, represents a kind of protective mask that serves to set her apart from the poor and draw attention away from her domineering nature. Fascinated with the four "doggies," the children reach out to stroke them but their fascination soon turns to greed and greed to raw violence. Thoroughly frightened, Chepa "takes off the martens and throws them up in the air, in the midst of the group of children: they roar as they jump up to catch the skins and throw themselves to the ground, shouting, biting, that mass of writhing bodies that forget her." (p.164) Now unmasked and reduced to a terrified animal, Chepa whacks desperately at the children with her purse before falling exhausted on a trash heap.[18]

Chepa's traumatic incursion into the slums would seem to represent her descent into the labyrinthian maelstrom of her unconscious where symbolic images embodying the hidden, diabolical forces of domination and sexual desire surge forth to destroy her. Her climactic nightmare also depicts the conflicts and monstrous passions engendered by bad faith between individuals,[19] as well as by generations of social injustice.

When Maya murders Violeta later that same night, he is more than likely transferring his animosity for Chepa to the weaker woman for whom he has no respect. He resents Chepa because she attempts to dominate his life but he also respects her and feels a strong sense of guilt for not having lived up to her expectations. Thus, by killing Violeta he not only destroys Chepa's power but also his own sense of guilt. [20]

Some of the most charming passages to be found in Donoso's entire literary production are those from *This Sunday* written from the point of view of the Vives' grandson, now a middle-aged man recalling experiences out of the distant past. Tinged with irony and nostalgia and strewn with symbols reflecting a child's vivid imagination, these passages provide the perfect contrast to the tense drama narrated by the plot's principal thread. For the grandchildren Alvaro and Chepa are diametrical opposites, the former sterile, aloof and absurd, and the latter generous, imaginative and loving. The family mansion, moreover, with its gardens, numerous rooms, closets and false doors, represents a paradise of stability and delight, a refuge closely identified with Chepa, where the youngsters can give free rein to their pent-up emotions. The narrator's attitude toward the large home is expressed symbolically at the beginning of the novel when he comes to spend the weekend with his grandparents. Crossing the city in his father's car during a storm he imagines himself enclosed in a fishbowl but ". . . arriving at my grandmother's house was always like smashing the bowl without its being a crime, a chance to flow finally, to spill over." (p. 7) [21]

The five cousins' principal source of delight is the games they invent and play in the attic of the old mansion. Their favorite imaginary character is the seductive Mariola Roncafort, [22] queen of a handsome, immortal people called the Ueks. The enemies of the Ueks are an ugly, backward tribe named the Cuecos, whose perverse nature and intrigues lead to wars between the two nations. The battles are fought on a huge carpet decorated with medallions, one of which is occupied by the Ueks and another by the Cuecos. The Ueks' politicians and professional men, referred to as "Old Man-Old Men," are serious people who smoke cigars, know everything and resemble the children's fathers. In spite of Mariola's immortality, it is eventually decided the she must die so that she can be transformed into a goddess. Chepa leads the tearful funeral procession on Sunday morning, the intention being to resurrect the mythical heroine the following week. "But there was no next Sunday. Sundays in my grandmother's house were suspended and Mariola Roncafort, like any other woman of flesh and blood, was dead forever." (p. 170)

The demise of Mariola and the tragic events of "this Sunday" mark the end of a world of innocence, delight and fantasy. It should be pointed out, however, that the children's games also parody the milieu which is beginning to mold their lives. The beautiful, eternal Ueks and the ugly, perverse Cuecos represent rigid social categories that have already taken shape in their minds, categories that are illuminated symbolically by the previously mentioned medallions decorating the attic rug. [23] The Old Man-Old Men, moreover, bring to mind the wealthy bourgeois leaders of the existentialists' "serious world" whose positions the youngsters are destined to occupy.[24]

This Sunday is an ingeniously structured novel whose central action occurs within a time frame of less then twenty-four hours.[25]

Three short sections narrated by the Vives' grandson appear at the beginning, the end, and midway through the book which contains, in addition, two principal parts, the first dealing primarily with Alvaro and Violeta and the second with Chepa and Maya. Alvaro's youth and Chepa's relations with Maya prior to his brief appearance on Sunday morning are related through a series of adroitly arranged flashbacks that tend to abolish lineal causality and create an impression of dynamic movement. These tendencies are enhanced by the frequently shifting point of view which negates the notions of omniscience and absolute truth. The characters are presented through a series of interreacting reflectors: Chepa and Violeta are seen through Alvaro's consciousness, Alvaro and Maya through Chepa's, and both Alvaro and Chepa through their own interior monologues. An additional dimension to the personalities of Alvaro and Chepa is provided by their grandson-narrator whose irony and nostalgia sharpen contrasts, soften harsh realities and create ambiguity.

The abrupt broadening and narrowing of the narrative perspective is often utilized as a means of heightening dramatic effect and inducing reader involvement. For example, in the following passage the grandson recalls the habitual Sunday dinners in the Vives residence and then an incident that occurred on one specific occasion. Initially the paragraph is rendered in the past tense in the form of narrative summary, but suddenly it veers to the present to record the vivid verbal exchange of the ensuing scene.[26] This technique of juxtaposing past with present and summary with scene thrusts the distant observer into the very midst of the action, highlighting the events and eliminating temporal and spatial boundaries with maximum brevity.

On Sunday, at those intricate family luncheons where we ate Violeta's famous *empanadas*, he [the grandfather] occupied the head of the table . . . always remaining silent in the midst of the discussions and the gossip, eating the tasteless, colorless foods that would not hurt his delicate stomach. And for dessert he ate only white gelatin in the form of a star: always the same, all the Sundays of my childhood. There at the far end of the Sunday table . . . my grandfather's face . . . swallows those translucent, shivering stars . . . And I, at the other end of the table, cry and stamp my feet because I do not want cantaloupe . . . I want a star . . . tell Grandpapa to give me a star, I want and I want . . . and I throw my spoon into the center of the table and my mother gets up and comes to scold me because I am bad . . . No, not bad, spoiled, because he is an only child . . . The "no" of my grandmother is persuasive and absolving: no, bring the child a star so he won't cry . . . And she herself . . . cuts a sliver of the star and puts it in my mouth . . . it does not taste like a star, and I spit it onto my napkin, which is embroidered with little ducks, and then they take me shrieking from the dining room . . . (p. 9)

Although to a lesser extent than in *The Obscene Bird of Night*, Donoso utilizes the stream-of-consciousness technique in *This Sunday* with notable success. These slices of interior life, several of which have already been quoted above, interpret the characters' thoughts as they occur in their original raw stage prior to grammatical articulation and lend an additional dimension to the fictional portrait by blending interior with exterior experience.[27] The stream-of-consciousness technique usually makes use of free association as a means of providing greater insight into the character. For example, at the beginning of part one, Alvaro notices a chip on a tea pot that reminds him of the mole on Maya's lip, which in turn evokes his terror of death caused by what he fears is a cancerous mole on his chest. Other interior monologues furnish pertinent information about past events, a case in point being Alvaro's mental return to his youth unleased by the smell of Violeta's *empanadas*.

Chepa's relations with Maya provide some of the best stream-of-consciousness passages as, for example, when she informs him she has at last secured his parole. The first sentence of the emotionally charged paragraph quoted below can be seen as a simple statement by an omniscient narrator. The second sentence focuses initially on Chepa's particular field of vision ("Then he threw himself down from the ceiling to her knees . . ."), but the author is speaking, referring to Chepa in the third person ("she felt uncomfortable . . ."), which initiates an indirect interior monologue. It is impossible to tell whether the phrases "Fanny would laugh . . . she would laugh" are phrased directly by Chepa or interpreted by the author, but the final clause of the sentence ("what I've just given him.") obviously emanates from Chepa's psyche. The rest of the paragraph constitutes a direct interior monologue with its first-person point of view and its pulsating movements reflecting the character's internal rhythms of thought and sensory impressions prior to organization in traditionally structured syntax. The fluid state of Chepa's mind is also conveyed by rhetorical devices such as the repetition of *and* and the use of present participles (pressing, imprisoning, caressing, crying) to impart a feeling of immediacy.

He focused his gaze and looked down at her. Then he threw himself down from the ceiling to her knees and sunk his head in her lap and she felt uncomfortable with that man who was crying, who wanted to embrace her, and Fanny would laugh and who knows what she would say . . . but it doesn't matter because Maya is free and he's crying and no one has ever given him what I've just given him. It's as though he were born again, and he realizes it, and I can't stop touching him, yes, his black bristled head and his neck, and it feels terribly hard and terribly strong, the rough, warm skin of those hands that are so small pressing and imprisoning hers . . . what does anything matter, caressing the head of that man who is crying into her skirt. (pp. 115–116)

The morning of Maya's release when Chepa arrives at the prison to take him to Violeta's home, a guard informs her that Maya has already left with Marujita Bueras. Angry, humiliated and disappointed, Chepa drives through a nearby park, her mind seething with conflicting emotions, desultory images and intimate reflections on her personal life. The abrupt temporal dislocations and shifting perspectives, which include the ominiscient narrator's point of view and both the direct and indirect interior monologues, capture the multidirectional movement of her psyche and lend possible insight into the complex currents underlying her outward behavior.

It was easy to say to herself as she got into the car, "Goddamned ungrateful tramp," and forget him. But that wasn't the problem . . . Now she was like someone blindfolded, with a sort of cramp that prevented her from starting the motor: she didn't know what to do, where to go . . . No, not to the park. . . . Go to Marujita's. . . . She couldn't do it because she was a lady: this lady . . . peering at the couples veiled by the new greenery of the willows beside the lake. Maya and Marujita. . . . She ought to return home . . . See that they make the gelatin molds for Alvaro. . . . And the children who are coming to the house tomorrow . . . and I don't want to see them because they belong to their parents, not to me, nobody belongs to me but Maya . . . and I am his eyes and . . . his dreams . . . I was. I was all of this. Because now that he's not inside he doesn't need any eyes but his own . . . Maya's contracted hand . . . on Marujita's perm in the bed of that room . . . But no. Stop it. I don't envy sexual things. God knows that Alvaro began to kill that in me within a month of being married . . . She envied other things. Being with him. Today. . . . Watching for him. That is Maya, that one who is embracing Marujita beside the huge forsythia . . . look Maya. . . . I'll wait for you here on the corner . . . then I will call them: get into the car, children, I'll take you both for a ride . . . (pp. 126–28)

Like Donoso's other works, *This Sunday* utilizes symbols, recurring motifs, foreshadowing devices, parallels, and contrasts in order to highlight themes and establish compositional balance. The frequently-alluded-to mole on Maya's lip marks him as a victim of social deterministic forces such as poverty and mental illness over which he has no control, while Alvaro's mole symbolizes the destructive influence of Chepa, an idea suggested by the juxtaposition of his strong resentment of her and his terror of cancer. The slum children fighting over Chepa's fur piece dissolve into a "mass of writhing bodies" (p. 164), but even more grotesque is a somewhat similar image, on the final pages of the novel, of a group of urchins who take refuge in the dilapidated Vives mansion. "Their ragged bodies mingled on the floor with the bodies of their mangy dogs form a single strange animal, like something invented from our fantasies in those days, with many heads, a variety of skins and extremities." (pp. 176–77)[28] Like Maya's and Alvaro's moles, these descriptions of violence and misery further illuminate the disastrous results of unbridled passion, irrationality and injustice.

The *empanadas* Alvaro brings home from Violeta's house every Sunday constitute the basis for a ritual in his life, providing him with the illusion of cyclical renewal and thus a means of warding off the terror of death and nothingness. These meat pies also symbolize the regenerative power of the Eucharist which in Alvaro's case turns out to be ironic in view of his despair and agonizing end only five months after the events of "this Sunday."

Numerous passages in the novel foreshadow subsequent occurrences, thereby helping to link episodes and enhance aesthetic unity. At the beginning of part I the chip in Alvaro's teapot reminds him of a mole on the face of "someone I don't know very well and whom I don't care for" (p. 19), a thought that anticipates Maya's appearance six pages later. An insight into Maya's character is also provided when Chepa, seeing him for the first time, thinks he is playfully chasing another inmate in the prison patio, but her friend Fanny judges him more accurately. "Playing! Are you mad? He's a brute. Couldn't you see, if the other one hadn't bent down he would have knocked him out?" (p. 94)

Other episodes also anticipate the novel's tragic ending. Maya's confession to Chepa, "I swear, ma'am, that sometimes I feel like killing you because you're so good to me" (p. 139) turns out to be a foreshadowing of Violeta's murder which has also been prepared by her submission to both Alvaro and Maya. Finally Chepa's long illness prior to her death is augured in one of her interior monologues during the search for Maya in the shantytown. ". . . I don't want to keep on getting myself entangled. I'm tired of saving him. Of forgiving him. It's not what he needs. The only thing is to let Maya's black hand take hold of me, too, and then . . ." (p. 158) And just as she saw Maya lying in the prison infirmary with "his eyes fixed on the ceiling . . . blinking normally, like other people, only a little more slowly" (p. 95), Chepa, in her old age, is portrayed in bed "with her eyes fixed on the ceiling, blinking too regularly, too mechanically." (p. 173)

The many parallels and contrasts between characters and events in *This Sunday* also contribute to the book's remarkable symmetry. Mention has already been made of the children's amusing games which parody the adult world around them. In the attic of the Vives home a picture by the romantic French painter Puvis de Chavannes depicts a retinue of youths and maidens in a pine grove mourning over a corpse shrouded in white. Described toward the middle and at the end of the novel, the painting serves as an inspiration for the dramatic funeral in honor of Mariola Roncafort. This highly emotional event, brought about by the children's decision to have their heroine murdered at the hands of "a vile Cueco spy" (p. 169), is echoed on a more realistic level by Chepa's nightmarish "game" with the slum children and its frightful aftermath. For the remaining years of her life Chepa, along with all the delight and imagination she has embodied, is essentially as dead to her grandchildren as the deceased queen of the Ueks.

As products of a rigidly structured society, the four leading characters provide additional bases for the novel's unifying parallels and contrasts. In spite of the fact that they have nothing in common but their good looks and upper-class backgrounds, Alvaro and Chepa confidently exchange wedding vows. Their inability to love each other, however, proves fatal to their future happiness. After

several affairs with other women, Alvaro withdraws into himself, all
the while retaining fond memories of the sexual bliss he enjoyed in
his youth with Violeta. Chepa, on the other hand, attempts to escape from her "prison" through welfare work, eventually finding
herself strongly attracted to Maya. One of her interior monologues
describes the revitalizing effects of these associations which indicate
a mutual dependence between the sterile, cultured rich and the
more vital, instinctual poor.

Violeta belonged to Alvaro, as Maya belonged to her. Alvaro's smile was
almost spontaneous when Violeta was near. She had blossomed out while
working for Maya's release. Everyone told her so: Darling, you've taken off
ten years, what skin, what brightness in your eyes. (p. 119)

Not only the social structure, however, but also the characters'
psychological make-up contribute to the novel's symmetrical design
and dramatic development. Whereas Alvaro and Violeta represent
inertia—with no desire to change either their own lives or those of
others—Chepa and Maya attempt to alter their situations, the
former through domination and the latter through the acquisition of
wealth and social prestige. (Maya would like to have his suits made
by the same tailor who makes Don Alvaro's. Also on several occasions he tells Chepa that he longs to be in a position to eat at the
same table with Don Alvaro.) All four characters are eventually
destroyed by their weaknesses: Alvaro and Violeta through their
withdrawal or escape from freedom, and Chepa and Maya through
their denial of freedom to others.

The ending of *This Sunday* is beautiful, tragic and symbolic. An
image recurring throughout the book is that of the *animita* which,
according to a Chilean custom, is a candle lighted in memory of a
person who has died suddenly in an accident or been murdered.
The soul of the dead person is believed to hover over the site of his
death and if a candle is burned on that spot, the spirit will rise to
heaven and intercede with God for the person offering the candle.
Chepa's grandchildren are convinced she is destined to die "in an
accident or in a murder, or some other glorious way" (p. 81) and to
become a miraculous *animita*. Thus, after her death, when the
house is invaded by waifs who light fires at night to keep warm, the
nostalgic narrator relates these fires to both the *animita* legend and

his grandmother. He refuses, moreover, to take steps to prevent the conflagration the neighbors fear could occur.

> . . . I don't intend to say a word. I like the idea of those children taking refuge there, as if the house which was an extension of my grandmother's body were still alive: the cornucopia continuing to spill out. When they hand the house over to the wreckers they will open the doors and the windows. The light will come in as it did before. And they will find the house despoiled of doors and panels and door jambs and baseboards and parquets, a husk which will fall at the first blows of the pick into a pile of ruins in the garden overrun with weeds.
> But I would prefer it to end in a fire set by those children, a gigantic *animita* lit to her memory. (p. 177)

The *animita* not only portends Chepa's tragic fate, i.e., her violent confrontation with the slum children[29] and her symbolic death with Violeta's murder, but also embodies childlike fancy and delight, the aspect of Chepa the narrator wishes to preserve. The crumbling mansion recalls the "palace" or false-family symbol of "Veraneo" and, like the home of Misiá Elisa in *Coronation,* suggests a decadent society doomed to extinction. As in several of Donoso's other works, the collapse of human institutions and moral values leaves only imagination and beauty—embodied by the *animita* in *This Sunday*—to fill the void.

III *Conclusions*

In most respects *This Sunday* is a more satisfactory novel than *Coronation,* the author having abandoned intrusive rhetorical devices and sharpened his literary tools to define his themes, explore his subject matter and develop his characters. The result is a more objective, exacting scrutiny of complicated human relationships and their tragic repercussions. In spite of the fact that both works depict the nightmarish forces of instinct and irrationality lurking below the placid surface of the existing social order, *This Sunday* captures the explosive reality of the situation far more effectively than its predecessor. Obvious parallels exist between Andrés Abalos and Alvaro Vives—both withdraw from life and live in terror of death—but the latter is less contrived, more subtly drawn. The relationships between Andrés and Estela, on the one hand, and Chepa and Maya, on the other, though similar, are more complex and psychologically profound in the case of the second pair. Only Misiá Elisa measures up to her counterpart, Doña Chepa, both of whom represent memorable portraits.

Although *This Sunday* gives the initial impression of unstructured fluidity, its material is organized within a sharply outlined, artistically conceived framework. One of its most important accomplishments is its well-integrated mixture of realism and imagination, objective and subjective realities, and irony, and tragedy. The true secret of the book's unity, however, lies in its ingenious montage of past and present which not only conveys a simultaneity of the two temporal realms, but also underscores the loss-of-innocence theme that emerges from so many of Donoso's works. The reader of *This Sunday* might question whether it, like *Coronation*, strives too hard for compositional pattern and unity, a case in point being the identical symptoms of Maya's black hand and Chepa's final illness. Still Donoso's second novel is a finely wrought work of art exhibiting a firm equilibrium of authorial compulsion and control.

CHAPTER 4

Myth and the Absurd:
Hell Has No Limits

I *Plot and Mythical Allusions*

THE fact that *This Sunday* and *El lugar sin límites (Hell Has No Limits)* were published the same year (1966) perhaps explains some of their structural and thematic similarities. *Hell Has No Limits*, however, introduces a new concept of reality based primarily on myth, pervasive ambiguity, and elements of the absurd in the human experience. The setting of this somber, impeccably written novel is a house of prostitution located in a backwater, Estación El Olivo, whose founder and leading citizen is a wealthy politician-landowner named Alejandro Cruz (Don Alejo). The bordello is owned by an unattractive girl, Japonesita, and her homosexual father, Manuela, who dances for the customers. The reader gradually discovers that approximately twenty years earlier Japonesita had been conceived during a fiesta celebrating Don Alejo's election to the Senate. It seems that, as owner of the brothel, Don Alejo agreed to sign the property over to Big Japonesa (Japonesita's mother and at that time the manager) if she could seduce Manuela before the eyes of those present. Big Japonesa succeeded in winning the wager by promising to make Manuela her partner in the enterprise. Since Big Japonesa's death four years ago her daughter has operated the business which, like the town, is on the road to oblivion because, unknown to most of the inhabitants, Don Alejo has resolved to convert the entire area to vineyards. The plot reaches its climax with the long-anticipated arrival at the brothel of a truck driver named Pancho Vega, a latent homosexual whom both Manuela and Japonesita have been fearfully but hopefully expecting. As indicated below, the novel ends even more pessimistically than its predecessor.

Although the rural scene of *Hell Has No Limits* contrasts sharply

89

with the metropolitan setting of *This Sunday*, both works focus on a deteriorating house and false family as symbols of a decadent, feudal society comprised of exploiters and victims. The central action in each case occurs in less than twenty-four hours, on a Sunday, with frequent flashbacks inserted to give greater coherence to present events. Similar also are the manipulation of the point of view as well as other techniques discussed later in this chapter.

In *Hell Has No Limits* Donoso reinterprets Biblical and classical myths as a means of putting human situations and metaphysical concepts into new perspective. Indeed, the symbolic allusions to the Biblical myths of the Creation and the Fall provide a poetic framework for the depiction of an absurd world based at least in part on existentialist principles.[1] Don Alejo emerges as an archetypal god-figure who creates Estación El Olivo on land previously covered with vineyards, assuring the inhabitants of the community's bright future.[2] His subsequent election to the senate enhances his stature in the eyes of the townspeople, whose votes confirm their faith in his promises. He is portrayed not only as the most powerful person in the region, but also as omniscient and omnipresent, being fully informed of everything that happens and appearing, it would seem, from out of nowhere at the most opportune, or inopportune, moments. He is also said to be a kind-hearted man who looks like the "Good Lord, with his China-blue eyes and his snowy mustache and eyebrows." (p. 150)[3] And as Japonesa tells Manuela during the fiesta celebrating Don Alejo's election to the senate, "He's like God here in town. He does whatever he wants." (p. 189) Twenty years later the physical and moral stagnation in Estación El Olivo not only suggest its fall from grace, but also illustrate its degeneration into a kind of hell on earth, an absurd caricature of the paradise it was supposed to become.

II *The Absurd*

Jean-Paul Sartre believes that the absurd derives from modern man's loss of God, the denial of absolute values, and the pervasive feeling of having been cast adrift in the world without any visible reason for his existence. The resultant sense of freedom and responsibility imposed on man has led him to solitude, metaphysical anguish, and despair, important by-products of absurdity.

According to Albert Camus neither man alone nor the world by itself is absurd, but rather the absurd arises from the clash between reasoning man, on the one hand, striving for order, unity, and happiness and, on the other, the silent, unreasonable world offering no response to his persistent demands. The absurd man is one who recognizes a kind of void or lack of meaning in life and resolves to commit himself to the lifelong conflict between his intentions and the reality he encounters. Like Sisyphus in Greek mythology, who was condemned by the gods to roll a huge stone up a hill again and again for eternity and whom Camus considers the epitome of the absurd hero, the absurd man can attain heroic proportions by rebelling against his torment and by demonstrating that the struggle itself gives definition and joy to his existence. The absurd, then, is the metaphysical state of conscious man fully aware of inevitable death and nothingness; it is lucid reason pitted against chaos; it is the only certainty linking man with an alien world devoid of absolutes. Once man has recognized the absurd, Camus believes one must keep this awareness permanently alive by maintaining a constant state of revolt against ultimate defeat, this being his only means of achieving self-fulfillment and of transcending the tragedy of his existence. A denial of the absurd is seen as a form of bad faith, self-evasion, or escape from responsibility.

According to both Sartre and Camus the concept of the absurd restores man's freedom to live life to the fullest, liberating him from the bonds of preconceived, sacred values, and making fate a human rather than a divine matter. Suicide and faith in God (the "leap of faith"), then, are considered out of the question because either would represent an escape from the absurd, terminating the necessary state of tension between reasoning man and the unreasonable world. Both authors demonstrate an admiration for the human faculty of reason, but at the same time they also recognize its limits and, consequently, the impossibility of reducing the unintelligible world to rational principles. Sartre and Camus grant art a major role in the modern world, Sartre seeing it as a means of gaining immortality, and Camus as an absurd activity but, nevertheless, one that serves to enrich the meaningless world.

Although the French philosophers have defined and illustrated the absurd in the rational language of their essays and fiction, subsequent practioners of absurd literature have often relied on fantasy and other antirational devices to present their perceptions of life without purpose. Some of these writers, including Samuel Beckett, Eugène Ionesco, Jorge Luis Borges and Julio Cortázar, have attacked reason more forcefully, and probably more effectively, than either Sartre or Camus.

In *Hell Has No Limits* Donoso depicts an absurd, paradoxical world of myths and rituals camouflaged by grotesque distortions. His intentions are to undermine traditional values, reveal the bankruptcy of reason, and jar the reader onto new levels of awareness by exposing the other side of reality. Thus, in his novelistic universe a poverty-ridden, isolated village represents man's world in microcosm, a ramshackle bordello his abode, and a sexual deviate, a prostitute and a selfish, frigid virgin the members of his household. A metaphor of this decadent social organization, the bordello is described as follows:

The house was sinking. One day they realized that the sidewalk was no longer even with the dirt floor, but higher, so they tried to check it by installing a stone slab, with two wedges, in the doorway. It was no use. As the years passed, the sidewalk . . . rose almost imperceptibly, while the floor was sinking. . . . The stone slab . . . had never been level and now its cracks collected burnt matches, mint wrappers . . . toothpicks, lint, and buttons. Sometimes grass sprang up around the edges. (p. 154)

The themes of the Fall and the absurd are reinforced by the characters, whose adverse fate and physical and psychological ambiguities annihilate hope and nullify rational absolutes. Don Alejo, for example, is not only a benign god-figure who creates Estación El Olivo and gives hope to its inhabitants; he is also a corrupt politician, a carouser, and the symbolic representative of an evil deity who exploits his fellow men and plots the destruction of the town, ". . . all for some incomprehensible purpose." (p. 181)[4] His prolonged domination has had a devastating effect on virtually every facet of the community, including its religious life. Catholic mass is held in a shed by a priest who appears blear-eyed, only on Sundays, after having spent the previous night in a brothel. Though off limits, Don Alejo's estate has in a sense replaced the church as the sacred place in the minds of the townspeople, being separated from the other houses by a canal and having "a tall pine like a belfry" (p. 224) at its entrance. Manuela's family, moreover, owes its creation to Don Alejo's perverted scheme that makes a mockery out of Christian dogma and the concepts of love and marriage. And toward the end of the novel this absurd, omnipotent god-figure is obliged to face death, still thinking about the many projects he had planned to carry out on earth.

Further evidence of Don Alejo's ambiguous nature is provided by the other characters whose perceptions of him vary greatly. Although Manuela repeatedly sees him as a symbol of divinity, on one occasion she[5] calls him a heathen, and she also discerns his machinations to purchase the bordello in order to get her and Japonesita out of town. Big Japonesa looks up to Don Alejo as a superior being, but during the fiesta in honor of his election she confides in Manuela, "Now he's selling us land here in Estación, but I know him and I haven't fallen for it yet." (p. 189)

Don Alejo is alternately portrayed as old and feeble or big and powerful, occasionally even in the same scene. For example, when Pancho arrives at his home with Octavio to pay off the loan for his truck, "Pancho thought he (Don Alejo) looked so tall, as tall as when he used to look up to him, a boy barely up to his knees." Shortly thereafter Don Alejo "dropped into a rattan chair. . . . He looked small now. And sick." (p. 203)[6]

The landowner's evil powers are conveyed symbolically by his four vicious black dogs which frequently accompany him or are heard barking ominously in the vineyards. Carl G. Jung's discussion of the divine quaternity found in many religions offers a plausible, though by no means conclusive, explanation for these beasts, the number four signifying psychic completeness. According to Jung, there is an unconscious tendency at work to round off our trinitarian formula of the Godhead with a fourth element, the devil—[7] thus the evil side of Don Alejo. The four dogs also represent cyclical recurrence in time—and so a reflection of divine immortality and perennial evil—by the fact that their master has consistently kept the same number with the same names, identical in appearance, and always bred for their ferocity.

Japonesa is the only important character who lacks ambiguity, but her disillusion and death parallel the dramatic decline of Estación El Olivo and underscore the theme of the Fall. The center of Don Alejo's election campaign, Japonesa's bordello reaches its peak shortly thereafter when the conservative upper-middle class of landowners, administrators, and chief mechanics is approaching its heyday of material progress. At this time, we are told,

Japonesa didn't open her doors to just anybody. Only refined people. Only people with money in their pockets. That's why she belonged to don Alejo's political party, the historical, traditional, organized party, the party of decent people who paid their debts and stayed out of trouble, the people who

94

went to her house for amusement and whose belief that don Alejo would do great things for the region was as unshakable as Japonesa's. (p. 186)

However, instead of continuing to thrive as Don Alejo had promised, Estación El Olivo enters a period of decline which Japonesita recalls in the following monologue:

My mother died of grief. Grief because Estación El Olivo was going downhill . . . they said the paved road . . . was going to go right through El Olivo . . . But then they told her . . . that the road would only come within a mile and a half of the town, and then she began to lose hope . . . Big Japonesa remembered . . . how in the old days . . . .the elegant young men . . . would meet at sunset in front of the post office . . . The boys, so proper during the day . . . let their hair down at night at Japonesa's house, which never closed. And then just the road construction men came . . . and then . . . only common laborers from nearby . . . And later on, not even them. (pp. 171–72)

Through her physical abnormalities and dashed hopes, Japonesita also reinforces the novel's major themes. She is almost nineteen years old and the owner of a brothel, but she has yet to attain sexual maturity and is still a virgin. As the daughter of Big Japonesa and Manuela, she is the product of calculating ambition and pathetic insecurity and, perhaps for this reason, is thrifty to the point of stinginess. Her aspirations of buying a Wurlitzer phonograph to replace her rickety victrola are doomed from the beginning because, in spite of his words to the contrary, Don Alejo has never intended to allow electricity to be brought into Estación El Olivo. Moreover, when Japonesita's sexual desires for Pancho are finally aroused, the virile looking truck driver casts her aside in order to carouse with her father. The final irony of her existence occurs with the breakdown of her victrola, which underscores the discrepancy between her illusions and the reality of her situation. Japonesita finally resigns herself to a life without hope, rejecting the opportunity to move from the town even though it might disintegrate around her. Her existential attitude might be described as one of bad faith because she escapes from freedom by denying her potentialities as a free subject, accepting her role as a passive object of Don Alejo's domination and thus precluding any possibility of growth or change.

Pancho Vega is the novel's most fully developed character with the exception of Manuela. He is also the most paradoxical for, in spite of his muscular physique and virile appearance, he is both a coward and a latent homosexual. Possibly the illegitimate son of the domineering Don Alejo, he spends his youth on the landowner's estate which he views in retrospect as a paradise, even though he was obliged to attend school and was called a sissy for playing games with Don Alejo's daughter, Moniquita. Pancho emerges as a kind of fallen angel and symbol of evil when he turns out to be a very poor student and when he infects Moniquita with typhus, causing her death. He subsequently marries a strong-willed woman, fathers a child, and borrows money from Don Alejo in order to purchase a truck. Pancho's existential problem is a sharply defined conflict between his desires to sever all ties with his past and his longing for the security he enjoyed during his childhood on Don Alejo's estate. This yearning for freedom and unwillingness to assume the responsibility it entails form the basis for his anguish and, in Sartrean terms, illustrate man's desire to achieve omnipotence both as a free subject and a permanent object. [8]

The following passages depicting Pancho's last meeting with Don Alejo suggest man's mythical expulsion from the Garden of Paradise and the ensuing existential dilemma described above. The episode begins when Pancho receives money from his brother-in-law Octavio to make the final payment on the loan given to him by Don Alejo in order to buy his truck. As they drive along the road leading to the landowner's estate, Pancho recalls how he used to walk barefoot to school over the same ground until the tyrannical Don Alejo ordered him to go to work. These thoughts lead to his preoccupation with his daughter's education after which his smoldering fear and resentment of Don Alejo surface. "If I want to . . . I'll make my daughter study. Don Alejo has nothing to say about it . . . I'm my own boss . . . Now I'll pay the old man and leave for good." (p. 201)

When they approach the home of Don Alejo, the latter's four vicious dogs leap and growl at the truck, causing the anxiety-ridden Pancho to lose control of himself and give vent to his deeply ingrained hostility. "Then Pancho, because they made him angry . . . started to honk the horn like a madman and the dogs leapt higher scratching the red paint . . . but now it didn't matter, now nothing mattered except . . . honking enough to knock down the palm trees and the oak, to pierce the night . . ."(p. 201)[9]

While Octavio converses with Don Alejo on the porch, [10] Pancho

looks through the steamy dining room window and sees Misiá
Blanca, Don Alejo's wife, sitting at the table with one of her grand-
sons. Her blurred image reminds Pancho of how she looked "swimming in his tears" (p. 202) at the funeral of her daughter Moniquita,
whose memory evokes the pleasure he experienced in his childhood
when he used to play with the little girl. As he and Octavio drive
back to Estación El Olivo, Octavio convinces him that the ailing
Don Alejo has deliberately prevented electricity from being brought
into the town so that everybody will leave and he will be able to
cultivate the land again. The thought that all the familiar haunts of
his youth are about to disappear strikes terror into Pancho's heart,
not that he hopes to return to Estación El Olivo, but rather because
he wants to be able to remember it and "have it there in case." (p.
206) The certainty of don Alejo's approaching death, moreover,
"drained the night" and obliged the distraught truck driver to
"clutch the steering wheel to keep from falling into that abyss."
(p. 206)[11]

Pancho's actions in chapters ten and eleven bring the novel to its
major climax. Sitting in the gloomy atmosphere of the brothel an-
ticipating one final spree before the town's disappearance, he puts his
hand on Japonesita's leg, all the while evoking images of his truck, a
sexual symbol as well as an instrument of suicidal escape from unbearable freedom and aloneness.

He had paid off the whole debt and the truck was his . . . Caress his red
truck instead of Japonesita . . . and the harsh-voiced horn, just like
Daddy's voice Normita always said. His. More his than his wife. Or daughter. If he wanted . . . he could race it like a wild man, blowing his
horn . . . slowly pressing the accelerator to invade the depths of the night
and suddenly, just because, because don Alejo doesn't have any control
over me now, I could turn the wheel . . . enough to make the truck go off
the road, bounce and overturn and become a smear of silent, smoking iron
. . . Under his hand Japonesita's leg began to relax. (p. 216)

Pancho's sadistic and homosexual tendencies become more evident when, in a scene auguring the novel's brutal climax, he repulses Japonesita for Manuela and, in his imagination, converts her
(Manuela) into a lifeless object. "La Manuela's dance handles him
and he would like to grab her like this . . . sinking my hands into
her hot slimy viscera, clawing, leaving her flattened, harmless,
dead: a thing." (p. 221)

Manuela is perhaps Donoso's finest fictional creation, her grotesque ambiguity and her valiant struggle against fate constituting the novel's best examples of the absurd. Her artistic temperament and homosexuality are metaphors for her condition as an outsider, that of an alienated seeker of beauty and delight. A pathetic though independent figure prior to her arrival in Estación El Olivo, she feels imprisoned in the brothel where she is first dominated by the opportunistic Japonesa and later by her daughter, Japonesita. In this sordid environment, Manuela is the only person with the slightest sense of beauty, which she demonstrates not only by her singing and dedication to her art as a dancer, but also by taking charge of the decorations for the fiesta in honor of Don Alejo and by combing Japonesita's hair to make her more appealing to Pancho. The conflict between her lofty desires for love, light, and freedom, on the one hand, and her sexual inversion, advancing age (she is 60) and depressing material situation, on the other, evoke the absurd man's quest for order and unity in the unreasonable world.[12]

Manuela's sexual ambiguity gives rise to her frantic search for identity, contributing to the novel's mounting tension and further illustrating the theme of the absurd. For example, when Japonesita calls Manuela "father" and begs her father to protect her from Pancho, Manuela's exterior world seems to disintegrate, threatening to destroy her inner self as well.

Okay, okay, you crappy girl, then don't call me father. Because when Japonesita called him father, the flamenco dress [a symbol of femininity] over the washstand looked older, the percale threadbare, the red faded . . . and the long, cold, dark night reaching through the vineyards, clutching, choking this spark that had been cultivated in the deserted town, don't call me father, empty-headed bitch. Call me la Manuela . . .

. . . .
But then Japonesita would suddenly call him that and his own image would blur as if a drop of water had fallen on it and then he'd lose sight of herself, himself, myself, I don't know, he doesn't know, he can't see la Manuela anymore and there's nothing, this anguish, this helplessness, nothing else, this enormous blot of water in which he's shipwrecked. (pp. 175–76)

Manuela's identity crisis is intensified by her awareness of death which will nullify her aspirations of professional grandeur and, ironically, preserve for posterity only her masculine identity.

. . . one fine day she, who could have been the princess of . . . all the whorehouses in the province, she would kick the bucket and the old woman of death would come to carry her off forever . . . and they would bury her in a niche in the San Alfonso cemetery under a stone that would say, 'Manuel González Astica' and then . . . no one in the whole area . . . would remember that the great Manuela was lying there. (p. 182)

When Pancho arrives at the brothel with Octavio, the terror stricken Manuela flees to the henhouse where, shivering with cold, she yearns to participate in the festivities. Her daughter's sudden call for help ("ay, ay, papa" p. 208) unleashes an interior monologue in which she relives her sexual experience with Big Japonesa twenty years previously, the only time in her life she has had intercourse with a woman. This passage, one of the finest in Donoso's writings, mocks the traditional concept of the sexual act and demythicizes God's (Don Alejo's) role therein. Thus Manuela recalls that while Don Alejo and his friends watched them through the window, she found herself

smothered in that flesh, that drunken woman's mouth searching for mine the way a pig roots in a swamp . . . this woman who was reminding me that the house was going to be mine . . . and don Alejo watching us . . . they're betraying me. . . . it was a betrayal to capture me and lock me up in jail forever . . . that body with its unimaginable incomprehensible channels and caverns . . . and that boiling so different from mine, my foolish doll's body . . . dead in her arms . . . I hear laughter in the window; don Alejo . . . watching us writhe . . . to humor him because he ordered it and this is the only way he'll give us this adobe house . . . No honey, Manuela as if we were two women, look, see, our legs wound together, sex in sex, two identical sexes . . . no, no, you're the woman, Manuela, I'm the man, look how I'm taking off your panties and loosening your brassiere . . . and I feel her heat devouring me, me, a me that doesn't exist . . . (pp. 209–10)

Orgasm thrusts Manuela into a web of confusion from which she is still—twenty years later—trying to extricate herself.

. . . and she [Big Japonesa] says into my ear . . . my sweet girl, my sweet boy. . . . We can't tell anybody, I'm ashamed of what happened, don't be silly, Manuela, you won the house royally . . . for the two of us. But swear never again, Japonesa, oh God how disgusting, swear to me, partners yes, but this no, never again because what I'm needing so much now no longer exists, that you and that me, I'd like so desperately to call to from this corner of the henhouse, while I watch them dance, there in the parlor . . . (p. 211)

A continuation of this interior monologue expresses Manuela's dreams of femininity, artistry and professional glory.

Papa. What do you mean papa . . . Nobody's papa. I'm just plain Manuela, the one who can dance until dawn and make a roomful of drunks laugh . . . while she, the artist, receives applause, and the light bursts into an infinity of stars . . . on the stage, with a flower behind her ear, as old and knock-kneed as she is, she's still more woman than all the Lucys and Clotys and Japonesitas on the face of the earth . . . arching her back and pursing her lips and tapping furiously, they'd laugh harder and their wave of laughter would carry her up, up into the lights. (pp. 211–12)

Eventually Manuela dons her flamenco dress, but her fluctuating identity set forth in the following passage indicates the fragile nature and terrifying ambiguity of the human personality which, under the onslaught of emotions, is subject to fragmentation.

He takes off his shirt . . . He removes his pants and he's naked . . . that foreign thing hanging from him. He puts on the Spanish dress . . . She adjusts the bodice . . . a little padding here where I don't have any-thing . . . because I'm so tiny, a dainty little gypsy girl . . . that's why she doesn't have breasts, almost like a little boy, but she's not, she's feminine, with her curved figure and all . . . She's just the great artist . . . she's a fag, she wants to amuse herself . . . If only I were younger . . . my joints hurt . . . I feel like staying in bed forever . . . (p. 212)

In the final climactic lines of this episode Manuela emerges as a grotesque parody of the consummate performer she strives to represent. Her valiant efforts to overcome the absurdity of her situation, however, negate her torment and constitute her grandeur. With a flower in her hair, she

walks across the patio . . . So skinny, dear God, no one's going to like me, especially with my stained dress and muddy feet and she removes a vine leaf clinging to the muck on her heel and goes toward the light . . . she hides behind the door, listening, while she makes the sign of the cross as all great artists do before walking into the light. (pp. 212–13)

While Manuela is still hiding, it is rumored that Don Alejo is on the point of death and that his fierce dogs, whose barking is heard in the vineyards, are running loose. The dying fiesta is enlivened by Manuela's dance after which she begs Pancho to take her away "to see a bit of light" (p. 221). As they leave the brothel accompanied by Octavio, Manuela makes the mistake of kissing Pancho and the latter, fearing his brother-in-law will discover his homosexual tendencies, retaliates by striking Manuela who breaks away and runs toward Don Alejo's home calling for help: "don Alejo promised he would be all right, that he would take care of him . . . it was a promise . . ."[13] (pp. 223–24) Manuela is overtaken by her two pursuers on the banks of the Palos canal near the "tall pine like a belfry" (p. 224) which looms high above the surrounding oak trees. The ensuing struggle constitutes a memorable scene characterized by grotesque sadism and punctuated by metaphysical irony.

Octavio . . . started lashing at him with fists . . . their hot bodies writhing, gasping over la Manuela who could no longer scream, their heavy, stiff bodies, the three of them one sticky mass squirming like some fantastic, three-headed animal with multiple limbs, wounded and seething, the three fused there in the grass by vomit and heat and pain . . . punishing him, her, them, shuddering gratifications, excruciating confusion, la Manuela's frail body resists no more . . . can't even moan from the pain, hot mouths, hot hands, slavering, hard bodies wounding his, bodies that howl and insult and grope, that monster of three tortuous bodies, breaking and tearing . . . until nothing is left and now la Manuela scarcely sees, scarcely hears, scarcely feels . . . and they escape through the blackberry bushes and she is left alone by the river that separates her from the vineyards where don Alejo waits, benevolent. (pp. 224–25)

In the final chapter Japonesita is left in the bordello with Don Céspedes, Don Alejo's old night watchman, who describes the landowner's strange actions of the previous evening ("he kept walking around and around, looking at everything as if he wanted to fix it all in his mind . . . until . . . he turned the dogs loose in the vineyard." p. 226) Japonesita has given up all hope, preferring tranquility to expectations of change. In reply to Don Céspedes' question about Manuela's fate, she describes her father's numerous past escapades with men like Pancho and his inability to mend his ways in spite of his repeated pledges to do so. After the old man's departure, Japonesita bolts the door, extinguishes the lamps, and retires. The howling of Don Alejo's dogs, the muffled sobs of a prostitute's child and the blackness of night juxtapose final impressions of impending doom, pathetic helplessness, and oblivion.

Manuela emerges as the novel's only absurd hero. Unlike Big Japonesa and Japonesita, who resign themselves to their fate, and unlike Pancho, who denies his freedom and responsibility through cowardice and sadism, Manuela maintains an attitude of revolt against her adverse reality in spite of her awareness of defeat in the form of death and nothingness. Contrary to the absurd hero, however, she makes the mistake on at least two occasions of putting her trust in the god-figure, Don Alejo, each time with disastrous results. On the first occasion her trust in the influential senator motivates her to accept Japonesa's offer of a business partnership, a decision that leads to her "imprisonment" in the brothel. (. . . "if it's true this town's on its way up, maybe life won't be so bad, and there's hope even for an ugly fag like me, and then my misfortune wouldn't be a misfortune but would turn to a miracle thanks to don Alejo . . .", p. 198). Still, even though her "leap of faith" would be condemned by the existentialists as an irrational escape from responsibility, in Manuela's case it serves to heighten the ambiguity of her character and the absurdity of her destiny.

Manuela's flight from Pancho and Octavio and its horrible aftermath evoke modern man's vain search for the missing God and the tragedy of being left to his own devices in the violence-ridden, unreasonable world. In this conceptual framework Don Alejo embodies a wicked deity who not only remains indifferent to human suffering, but even turns his dogs loose to perpetuate evil and destruction on the eve of his death. The "tall pine like a belfry" Manuela catches sight of during her flight alludes ironically to a religious faith unwarranted by the terrible destiny awaiting all men. The absurdity of her fate, moreover, is conveyed by the grotesque, three-headed monster which represents the dehumanizing forces of irrationality as well as the retrogression to chaos and formlessness.[14]

There is some evidence that Manuela embodies an ironic Christ-figure whose sexual ambiguity casts terrifying doubts on the *machismo* myth,[15] thus making it necessary for her to be sacrificed in order to preserve the rigid categories she threatens to undermine. As she tells Japonesita after being thrown into the canal during the fiesta honoring Don Alejo, "I'm used to it. I don't know why they . . . do this . . . to me when I dance, it's as if they were afraid of me. I don't know why if they know I'm just a fag." (p. 196) And twenty years later, just as Christ was allowed to be sacrificed on

Calvary, Manuela is abandoned by the silent god-figure, Don Alejo, when she exposes Pancho Vega's sexual ambivalence and is submerged into the maelstrom of human passions. If Manuela is indeed intended to represent a Christ-figure, her terrible struggle with Pancho would seem to symbolize the apocalyptic struggle between Good and Evil, or between Christ and Antichrist.

Manuela also communicates the eternal value of art which provides a means of revolt against the unreasonable world and the only salvation from the abyss of absurdity. As Pancho indicates just before Manuela comes forth from the henhouse to enliven the fiesta, "It can't be all so damn sad in this town don Alejo's going to tear down and plow under, surrounded by vineyards that are going to swallow it up . . . I want to have fun, that nutty Manuela has to come out and save us . ." (p. 219) And shortly thereafter she appears on the platform in her "glowing dress" to amuse them and "kill dangerous, mercurial time that wants to devour them." (p. 220)

Manuela's grotesque ambiguity and heroic efforts to give meaning to her existence by creating her own set of values make her an unforgettable metaphor of the absurd human condition. She also emerges as a tragic victim of irony because, although she is sincere and utterly without malice, she must suffer an unjust fate, more horrible than she has any reason to expect.

III   *Structure and Technique*

The pessimistic view of man and his institutions set forth in *Hell Has No Limits* is countered by the novel's aesthetic realization which includes a remarkable degree of structural unity. The first five of the twelve chapters occur in linear form between early Sunday morning and late that same evening when Manuela and Japonesita hear Pancho's truck approaching the brothel. Chapters six and seven consist of flashbacks relating the celebration of Don Alejo's election to the Senate and the wager resulting in the conception of Japonesita. Chapter eight deals with Pancho's visit with Don Alejo in order to pay off his debt, after which he and Octavio head for Japonesita's house, thus repeating the final lines of chapter five from a different perspective. Chapters nine and ten narrate events that occur on parallel temporal planes, each unit terminating with the anticipation of Manuela's flamenco dance, and the last two chapters depict Manuela's dramatic performance, her struggle with Pancho and Octavio and the somber ending. Thus, except for chapters six

and seven, which are essential to both plot and thematic development, the central action zigzags forward, postponing climactic
events, accumulating emotional momentum, and heightening the
impact of the final chapters.

Within this orderly, fundamentally lineal framework, Donoso
utilizes a wide variety of techniques designed to intensify dramatic
effect and capture the moral confusion and lack of absolutes in today's world. The novel is composed principally of dramatic scenes
and descriptions which are frequently vivified by shifting points of
view and abrupt changes in verbal tenses. Although summaries by
an omniscient narrator serve occasionally to broaden perspective,
enhance understanding or accelerate movement, the use of this
traditional method is held to a minimum. Instead, Donoso often
penetrates the minds of his characters, interpreting their thoughts
and fleeting impressions on various levels of consciousness, and
then withdraws to view them briefly from an exterior angle. The
novel's opening lines blend Manuela's external reality with snatches
of her unexpressed reflections:

La Manuela forced open her bleary eyes, stretched briefly and
. . . reached for the clock. Five to ten. Eleven o'clock mass. Sticky films
again sealed her eyes as she put the clock back . . . Half an hour at least
before her daughter would ask for breakfast. She ran her tongue over her
toothless gums: hot sawdust, and breath like rotten eggs. From drinking so
much new wine . . . She felt a shiver—of course!—she opened her eyes
and sat up in bed: Pancho Vega was in town. She covered her shoulders
with the rumpled pink shawl from her daughter's side of the bed. (p. 149)

Although the third-person reflector or viewpoint character is successfully utilized in the earlier works in order to sharpen the narrative perspective and partially nullify omniscience, the use of this
technique has been considerably expanded in *Hell Has No Limits*.
Thus, not only are the descriptions of characters and events filtered
through individual minds,[16] but, as illustrated by the following quotations, even the novel's setting is viewed through the eyes of Manuela, and the latter's first appearance in Estación El Olivo is conveyed by a collective third-person-plural reflector, the women of
the town:

. . . she [Manuela] looked up the street toward the poplar grove that
marked the edge of town, three blocks away . . . She hurried past the

houses . . . Very few were occupied because the coopers moved their bus-
inesses to Talca long ago . . . Further on . . . more brambles and a canal
separated the town from don Alejandro's vineyards. La Manuela stopped
. . . to look at them . . . Vineyards, as far as the eye could see. (p. 155)

   That morning they [the women of the town] had seen the three Farías
sisters step off the train from Talca . . . and a man, if you could call him
that. The women . . . discussed what he might be: skinny as a broomstick,
with long hair, his eyes were made up almost as much as the Farías sisters'.
(p. 183)

   Fictional material imparted through the consciousness of a third-
person reflector is likely to be more believable than that related by
an omniscient narrator outside the story. In the case of *Hell Has No
Limits*, moreover, this technique tends to isolate each individual
character, underscore the theme of alienation, and, through the
presentation of multiple reflectors, demonstrate the unattainability
of any single version of the truth. The resulting ambiguity becomes
even more pervasive through the skillful use of the stream of consciousness which, as demonstrated in *This Sunday*, captures the
immediacy of events and enriches literary texture. The above-mentioned passage describing Pancho's visit with Don Alejo to pay off
his debt provides an illustration of the shifting narrative perspective, temporal dislocations, concrete imagery, and equivocal meaning conveyed by the uninhibited flow of unspoken thought patterns
characterizing this technique. In the following portion of the same
scene, which, it will be recalled, takes place at night on Don Alejo's
porch, Pancho's awareness of the landowner's conversation with
Octavio is blocked out when he catches sight of Misiá Blanca
through the dining room window. Her movements evoke from Pancho's memory a series of events from his childhood that give insight
into his character, help to explain his antagonism toward Don Alejo
and suggest man's mythical Fall. This symmetrically conceived
interior monologue is ended abruptly when the dining room light is
extinguished and Octavio's voice again becomes audible to Pancho.

They paced around the U of the porch. From time to time the image of
Misiá Blanca presiding at the long . . . table reappeared . . . within the
framed light of the window. Octavio was explaining something to don
Alejo . . . I don't want to hear it, he does it better than I do. . . . From a
plate Misiá Blanca selects a lump of toasted sugar. . . . One for her, one for
Moniquita and one for you, Panchito . . . go play in the garden, and don't

lose sight of her Pancho . . . you have to take care of her . . . he was the doll's father and she the mother, until the kids caught us playing with the little crib . . . sissy, sissy, playing with dolls like a girl and I don't want to ever come back but I have to . . . and I spy from the flower hedge . . . Until one day don Alejo sees me spying behind the flowers. I've caught you, you little bastard. And his hand grabs me here, at the neck, and I hang from his cape kicking, him so big and me so small . . . And he drags me through the bushes . . . who's going to take care of her except you . . . And I find her and touch her and from the tip of my body . . . my body drips something and wets me and then I get typhus and she does too and she dies and I don't . . . The dining room light has been turned off . . . Octavio's voice keeps explaining: yes, don Alejo, of course. (pp. 203–04)

Like Donoso's previous novels, *Hell Has No Limits* is replete with recurring themes, symbols and images that gradually acquire a kind of autonomy, illuminating content and creating movement, compositional pattern and ironic contrast. Some of the many examples include: Japonesita's pink shawl, which clashes with its colorless, sexually immature owner and accentuates her father's opinion that she is "all ambiguity" (p. 158);[17] Manuela's red Spanish dress, a symbol of femininity that masks her true sexual identity and elicits an emotional response from all those who witness her performance; the electric Wurlitzer, representing hope for Japonesita; the light for which Manuela yearns, symbolizing beauty and freedom; her resemblance to a bird, which conveys her desire to escape from the bordello as well as her fragility in the face of violence; Pancho's red truck connotating strength and virility; his recollection of Misiá Blanca's pantry filled with jars of fruit, an allusion to the "paradise" of his childhood; his incipient ulcer, a mark of his vulnerability to the domination of his wife and Don Alejo; Don Alejo's symmetrical vineyards, perhaps a paradigm of the structurally perfect cosmos he, as a deity, has created out of chaos; his benevolent blue eyes, white patriarchal mustache, and expensive vicuña cape; and his surname Cruz, meaning cross, an ironic allusion to the faith his actions nullify.

The ominous barking of Don Alejo's dogs and the honking of the horn on Pancho's truck emerge as paradoxical parallels, the former conveying the evil intentions of a venerated god-figure, and the latter, the threat of sexual violation by a timorous homosexual under the guise of a he-man. Through rhythmic repetition these two leitmotifs become mysteriously linked, modulating tonal quality, augmenting emotional impact, and imparting a vague notion that the characters' lives are determined by irrational forces outside the domain of cause and effect. Pancho's sadistic attack on Manuela and the latter's discovery of Don Alejo's indifference to her plight mark the culmination of the novel's confusion of opposites and ironic ambiguity.

The use of setting to create mood and reflect theme is extremely important in *Hell Has No Limits*, the prevailing atmosphere of gloom contrasting sharply with Manuela's yearning to be "singing, laughing, dancing in the spotlight every night forever." (p. 198) The many somber descriptions illuminated by flashes of light evoke the tenebrous paintings of the masters of chiaroscuro such as Caravaggio, Rembrandt, and Georges de la Tour.[18] These shadowy word pictures lend an additional spatial dimension to the novel and heighten dramatic effect by freezing poignant moments of time, a technique which also conveys the impression of impending doom and, as in the following example, focuses on the absurdity of life without purpose. It is a cold, dark night and Manuela has been combing Japonesita's hair in anticipation of Pancho's arrival. Her mood is one of dejection due to her fatigue and a morbid anticipation of death.

She touched her dress, wilted over the dirty potatoes . . . She saw herself in the mirror, over her daughter's face which gazed at itself ecstatically . . . the candles, on either side, were like those of a wake. Her own wake would have light like that . . . She was going to remain in Estación El Olivo forever. Die here, a long, long time before this daughter of hers who couldn't dance but was young and a woman whose hope, as she looked at herself in the broken mirror, wasn't a grotesque lie. (p. 177)[19]

IV   *Conclusions*

Hell Has No Limits is a more pessimistic and spontaneously conceived novel than its predecessors, and its ironic depiction of the Fall and poetic presentation of the absurd constitute its major ingredients. In Donoso's world, although man's desire for spiritual transcendence is denied him, he nevertheless seeks both the protection and the omnipotence of the missing God, a situation which, it turns out, is merely another form of the dependence-domination relationships prevailing among mortals. Modern, profane man, it would seem, retains vestiges of religious behavior which, when reactualized, are scarcely recognizable in their degenerated form. Inasmuch as human aspirations must end in defeat, man is a victim of absurdity or, as Sartre has stated, man is a useless passion.

Unlike the French existentialists, however, who seek to solve their dilemma through commitment to ideals and action, Donoso remains perilously close to nihilism, apparently, finding value only in the aesthetic perfection of his work. Indeed, even though Manuela is cruelly sacrificed to the forces of irrationality and evil, there are indications that her spirit may have been rescued from oblivion and preserved for eternity in the realm of poetic myth. Don Céspedes, Don Alejo's wiry old night watchman, bears certain resemblances to the mythical Charon who ferried the dead across the River Styx to Elysium, the island home of the blessed in Hades and the region through which the souls of the dead had to pass on their ascent to pure light.[20] In the final scene of the novel when Don Céspedes leaves the brothel to investigate the cause of the dogs' insistent howling, the reader may speculate that he will ferry Manuela's soul across the canal. The protagonist's yearning for light, then, would seem to suggest that she must pass through Elysium if she is to ascend to the illuminated kingdom of the gods.

The reader is also told in the last chapter that "the sky had cleared up around the moon . . . and the dogs were howling steadily at it, as if they were . . . begging it for something . . ." (p. 225) According to some versions of the classical myth, Elysium is located on the moon, leading one to speculate further that Don Alejo's dogs, the forces of evil, are begging the moon for Manuela's soul which is already out of reach in its ascent heavenward.

Although the corrupt feudal society described in *Hell Has No Limits* has its fictional base in Chile and Latin America, this aspect of the novel is merely a point of departure for its universal treatment of a decaying world in which human consciousness confronts the cruel reality of a metaphysical hoax. The book's mytho-poetic framework, aesthetic unity, and depiction of the absurd as the means of reaching the core of reality establish it as one of Donoso's two masterpieces, the other being *The Obscene Bird of Night*.

CHAPTER 5

The Obscene Bird of Night: *A Tribute to Consciousness*

I *The Plot*

WITH the publication of his most important novel to date, *El obsceno pájaro de la noche (The Obscene Bird of Night)*, 1970,[1] Donoso joins the ranks of those anti-novelists such as Carlos Fuentes, Julio Cortázar, John Hawkes, John Barth, Alain Robbe-Grillet, and Samuel Beckett who abandon traditional plot, character and thematic development in order to depict today's world in a more spontaneous and meaningful way.[2] Donoso's highly complex work, which combines many of its author's former preoccupations and obsessions, emerges as a showcase for an impressive array of styles and differs from its predecessors in its far greater degree of subjectivity. The grotesque fantasies, multiple identities, and disintegrating personality of the novel's central figure undermine conventional logic, convey a profound distrust of objective reality, and reflect the tragic condition of modern man threatened by the abyss of nothingness.

The narrator-protagonist Humberto Peñaloza is an indigent, aspiring young author who becomes the secretary and right-hand man of an influential politician, Don Jerónimo Azcoitía, owner of an estate called La Rinconada and of a rambling, church-operated home for the aged known as the Casa (Home). Other leading characters include Don Jerónimo's wife, Doña Inés de Azcoitía, and her crafty old servant, Peta Ponce. The plot describes the founding of the Casa, the wretched existence of its aged inhabitants, the bizarre relationships between the protagonist and the Azcoitía family, and life on La Rinconada where Don Jerónimo's deformed son, Boy, lives surrounded by other monsters employed to shield him from the world of normal human beings.

108

According to legend, the Casa was founded at some time in the remote past by a wealthy landowner as a convent-prison for his daughter who, along with her old nursemaid, was suspected of witch-craft. In reality, the religious retreat was constructed in the late eighteenth century by a rich widower named Azcoitía to provide a home for his daughter and establish a direct link between the Azcoitías and God, thus conserving the family's privileges in this life and the hereafter. The girl, Inés, is said to have saved the Casa from destruction during an earthquake by making the sign of the cross and offering her life to God. She died at the age of twenty "in the odor of sanctity."[3] Subsequently the Casa became a refuge for aging, upper-class citizens but, as it deteriorated, it eventually assumed its current function—that of a domicile for retired female servants of wealthy families and a storehouse for castoff belongings. At the present time only Don Jerónimo's pious wife, Doña Inés, takes an active interest in the crumbling institution, attempting to prevent its demolition and to obtain from the Pope the official beatification of Don Jerónimo's eighteenth-century ancestor, the blessed girl saint, Inés.

Another flashback relates Don Jerónimo's return from Europe during World War I, at which time his Uncle Clemente, a prominent ecclesiastical and political figure, convinces him to run for a conservative seat in Congress. Although at first reluctant to become involved in local affairs, Don Jerónimo quickly adapts himself to the rigidly stratified society, marries his beautiful cousin Doña Inés, and soon thereafter is elected to the Senate.

When Doña Inés fails to produce the long-desired offspring, she is beguiled by Peta Ponce, in a masterfully written and highly ambiguous episode, into having intercourse with Humberto and/or Don Jerónimo and subsequently gives birth to Boy. Don Jerónimo veiws the repugnant infant as "an incoherent cluster of reddish traits . . . chaos, disorder, a different but worse form of death" (p. 126) and feels abandoned by "the traditional powers from whom he and his forebears had received so many blessings in return for maintaining His order in the things of this earth." (p. 127) Thus the deformed child is left to be raised on La Rinconada which Humberto directs while attempting to write an historical biography of Don Jerónimo and his estate. Years later the young author-protagonist falls seriously ill with a bleeding ulcer for which he undergoes surgery and, convinced that his one-eyed physician Dr. Azula has removed eighty per cent of his organs, abandons La Rinconada to

take refuge in the Casa where he is nicknamed "Mudito." Meanwhile, the visibly aging Doña Inés, who resembles Peta Ponce more
and more each day, because of the transplanted organs she has
received from her servant, returns from her audience with the Pope
and moves into the Casa, ostensibly to devote her remaining years
to prayer. Instead, she sets about winning the tattered belongings of
the old women in a dog-racing game she plays with them and an
orphan prostitute named Iris Mateluna, believed to be the virgin
mother of a holy child. The bewildering, rapidly occurring events
discussed below bring the novel to its conclusion with the total
disintegration of the protagonist's visionary world.

II *Schizophrenia and Surrealism*

Although perhaps to a lesser degree than Donoso's other works,
The Obscene Bird of Night is anchored to Latin American reality, as
exemplified by its portrayal of a rigidly structured feudal society
whose selfish and corrupt upper class cannot exist without the poor
to command and exploit. The resulting domination and dependence
between masters and servants, at times ironically reversed, engender the complex, unhealthy human relationships of which the protagonist is a victim. Humberto Peñaloza's fantasmagorical world,
however, is the very antithesis of that portrayed by the realistic
social novel, emerging rather as a series of surrealistic visions generated by his schizophrenic mind. A literary movement which reacted
violently against the horrors of World War I, surrealism rejects the
tyranny of rationalism and, inspired by Freudian psychology, explores the subconscious through the depiction of dreams, states of
madness, and hallucinations caused by the use of drugs. Influenced
also by the Freudian method of free association, the surrealists prac-
ticed automatic writing as a means of breaking the fetters of reason
and capturing thoughts in their nascent state. Their principal goal
was the liberation and transformation of man which they hoped to
accomplish through the establishment of a direct link between the
objective and subjective realms and through the elimination of the
contradictions between the real and the imaginary.[4]

Humberto Peñaloza, the protagonist of *The Obscene Bird of
Night*, reveals many of the symptoms of schizophrenia, a mental
illness characterized by the disintegration of the personality, the
rational side of which becomes fragmented due to the invasion of
fantasies from the unconscious. As a means of protection against

imaginary dangers from without, the schizophrenic withdraws from reality and initiates an inward journey deep into the psyche, encountering fantastic symbolic images almost identical to those encountered by mythological heroes as well as by persons under the influence of drugs. Carl G. Jung calls these universal images archetypes of the collective unconscious, i.e., structures of the psyche that are not products of individual experiences, but rather of experiences common to all mankind.[5] In this world of fantasy the schizophrenic imagines himself to be free and omnipotent, his protection also taking the form of masks or personas[6] which can become a whole system of false selves often consisting of a patchwork of other people's personalities. The schizophrenic experiences an obsessive desire for participation with the world but at the same time is unable to conceive of a union with others without the terrifying loss of his own self. This fear of being engulfed by others precipitates his further withdrawal which in turn increases his terror of nothingness and triggers his renewed search for power and a sense of belonging. The schizophrenic often feels imprisoned within his isolated world of fantasy, a situation which can engender hostility among his grotesque split-off personalities and eventually reduce his visionary reality to ruins. In such cases the patient is also likely to regress in time, imagining himself to be an infant, a fetus in the womb, and even an integral part of the universe.[7]

Humberto Peñaloza's schizophrenic retreat from reality is more than likely initiated by his relationship with his strong-willed father, an impoverished schoolteacher whose deeply ingrained sense of social inferiority destroys his son's identity, but at the same time instills in him an overriding ambition. Humberto's first encounter with Don Jerónimo occurs when his father points out the imposing aristocrat on the street, an incident that kindles Humberto's desire for a mask in order to conceal his insignificance and achieve an illusion of power.

Then, as I watched you, Don Jerónimo, a gap of hunger opened in me and I wanted to escape through it from my own puny body and merge with the body of that man who was passing by, to become part of him, even if I were only his shadow, to merge with him or tear him apart completely, to dismember him and appropriate everything of his—his bearing, his coloring, the self-assurance with which he looked at everything without fear . . . because not only did he have everything but he was everything. I, on the

other hand, was nothing, nobody; that was something my father's stubborn
longing had taught me. (p. 80)[8]

One afternoon several years later Humberto is studying for a law
exam in the national museum of anthropology when the first split in
his personality occurs. While dreaming happily of achieving power
as a lawyer and judge, he gazes at a group of smiling mummies in a
fetal position which seem to reflect his own face but, at the same
time, suggest his retreat to the womb and nothingness. The reactions triggered by these extremes lead to the imagined appearance
of Don Jerónimo.

Their [the mummies'] smiles are my smile that smiles in the presence of
death, because I'm going to be such a big lawyer that I won't need the
ancient suns of the desert to preserve my features, and their smiles protect
me against any danger except the danger of seeing *him* [Jerónimo], dressed
in very light gray, standing behind me, observing the Atacameño mummies
without his face matching any of those smiles. I recognized him. He spoke
to me. I answered him. We walked together down the gallery . . . (p. 213)

A plausible explanation for what happens in the preceding passage is that 1) Humberto, too weak to stand alone, imagines a symbiotic union between himself and Don Jerónimo, who embodies
everything the young student lacks in order to fulfill his ambition for
omnipotence, and 2) Jerónimo becomes Humberto's persona or social mask. Subsequently Humberto's split personality breaks into
two additional subsystems, Boy and Mudito. The monster Boy
would appear to represent Jerónimo's shadow, i.e., what Jung has
called the vulnerable, unconscious side of the ego-personality, often
embodying those qualities that one dislikes most in other people. A
proud, handsome aristocrat, Don Jerónimo attempts to suppress his
shadow, a common psychological occurrence, by isolating Boy on La
Rinconada.[9]

The grotesque figures hired to live on the estate probably represent phantoms generated by Humberto's deteriorating mind, and La
Rinconada, Don Jerónimo's fortress against the forces of anarchy
and chaos embodied in Boy. Thus, the abnormal child is imprisoned
in a hermetically sealed limbo of rationalism where pain and pleasure are denied and education is based solely on visible reality. A
parody of Don Jerónimo's positivistic bourgeois world, this Kafkaesque realm of order, logic and material abundance evokes Goya's

well-known motto, "The sleep of reason produces monsters," which points to the dangers lurking in the unconscious and threatening to overwhelm the unwary rational ego.[10]

While living on La Rinconada, Humberto strives in vain to achieve omnipotence through his duties as director as well as through his creative activity, the historical biography which, for Donoso, represents the book that can drive an author mad. However, because he is the only "normal" person on the estate, Humberto suffers increasingly from isolation and paranoia, a situation that provokes his ulcer attack and results in his operation. His unforgettable surrealistic hallucinations immediately before and after the surgery[11] precipitate his flight to the Casa, indicating an abrupt shift to a lower level of consciousness and another phase of his retreat from reality, regression in time, and eventual descent into oblivion. A metaphor of this portion of Humberto's inner life, the dilapidated, labyrinthian Casa represents a kind of archetypal Jungian symbol of terror, ambiguity, and limitless possibilities, for it is here in the midst of the anarchic, domineering, and cabalistic crones that his schizophrenic fantasies of omnipotence and annihilation are realized through a bewildering proliferation of identities. Hermaphrodite and sexless, powerful and powerless, human and animal, man and deity, Humberto sees himself at various times as an aging, emasculated deaf-mute and servant (Mudito), one of the old women, Iris Mateluna's dog, an enormous head made of papier-mâché, a phallus, a bird, Iris' baby, Doña Inés' baby, Boy, a holy child destined to take the old women to heaven, a damp spot on the wall, a fetus, and, ultimately, an *imbunche*.[12]

Although the exploration of the unconscious realm in *The Obscene Bird of Night* is probably the novel's most obvious surrealistic element, other aspects of the movement are clearly in evidence. Like the surrealists, Donoso revolts against constraints imposed on man by outmoded conventions and seems to delight in mocking traditional beliefs and institutions. A case in point is a series of incidents involving Don Jerónimo's Uncle Clemente, a retired high-ranking ecclesiastic who first appears in chapter three when Mudito recalls the old man's final days spent in the Casa. His mental condition deteriorated steadily until he became violent and one day scandalized everybody by appearing naked in the presbytery where he began smashing everything in sight with his cane. Since his death the old ladies have been afraid to walk alone through the corridors after dark because they believe Don Clemente will chase them and they are too old to run. Convinced that he is condemned by God to wander about naked until sufficient rosaries are said for him to regain his clothing and enter the Kingdom of Heaven, they pray that God will return his shoes, cassock, and shorts, "yes, his underpants are the most urgent." (p. 44) In spite of their prayers, however, Don Clemente has received only his socks and undershirt.

This humorous passage acquires ironic significance when in a flashback in chapter ten, Don Clemente makes his second appearance as an aging but still alert civic leader proclaiming the political platitudes of the arrogant upper-class in his efforts to convince his nephew to become a candidate for the Conservative Party and thus help preserve the sacred values that are being threatened: "I won't have you saying that your country's politics don't interest you. It's blasphemy. It means that upstarts and opportunists, all kinds of unbelieving radicals, will upset the foundations of society such as God created it, when He vested authority in us. He divided fortunes as He saw fit, giving the poor their simple pleasures, placing on our shoulders the obligations that make us His representatives on earth. His Commandments forbid violence against His divine order, and that's exactly what this bunch of unknowns, this rabble, is up to." (p. 141)

Far more iconoclastic is a series of grotesque and, at times, hilarious episodes which parody Christian myth and, like much antiliterature, utilize the irrational and the absurd to attack the falsity of conventions. In these scenes, replete with pungent naturalistic details, the aging Damiana and Mudito become the dolls of Iris Mateluna, the pregnant "virgin" prostitute. While awaiting the birth of the miraculous baby who will assure them salvation in heaven, the old women hover around Iris, watching her nurse her "babies" and retelling old wives' tales concerning the care of infants. When the holy child is born, it turns out to be Mudito whom Iris eventually uses as a pawn in the dog-racing game she plays with Doña Inés. Betting Mudito against Doña Inés' false teeth, she loses, whereby Doña Inés assumes the identity of the holy virgin and Iris is scorned as a prostitute. When Mudito, now Doña Inés' baby, is put in bed with her, his attempt to seduce her provokes an attack of madness and she is carried off to a mental hospital in a straitjacket.

In *The Obscene Bird of Night* ambiguity serves as an antidote for reason which, like the surrealists, Donoso considers a barrier to freedom of imagination. One of the most ambiguous passages deals with the act of love by which Boy is conceived, an incident Mudito recalls many years later as he lies ill in the Casa comforted by Mother Benita. It seems that Humberto had been shot in a mining community during Jerónimo's election campaign when somebody mistook him for his employer. Feverish from his wound and imagining that his identity had fused with Jerónimo's, Humberto returned alone to La Rinconada where he was met by Doña Inés. The latter, desperate because she was still childless after five years of marriage, had been advised by Peta Ponce that in order to conceive she should bring Don Jerónimo to her (Peta Ponce's) room to have intercourse on her bed. Inasmuch as Don Jerónimo would have nothing to do with his wife's servant, Doña Inés arranged to have Humberto meet her in Peta Ponce's room where the old woman would treat his wound. During the ensuing sexual act Doña Inés consistently addressed Humberto as Jerónimo but refused to allow any part of his body to touch her other than his sex organ. Upon his return to La Rinconada, Jerónimo went to bed with his wife and soon thereafter heard a yellow bitch howling at the moon under their window. Ignoring Doña Inés' protests, he turned loose his four ferocious dogs so that they could tear the yellow bitch to shreds and put an end to "her dialogue with the accomplice moon." (p. 180)[13]

As soon as it became known that Doña Inés was pregnant, Humberto asked the gardener if he ever found the carcass of the yellow bitch. His negative reply led Humberto to speculate as follows: Perhaps Doña Inés went to Peta Ponce's room to meet Humberto while Peta Ponce, having assumed the identity of the yellow bitch, howled under the window and caused Don Jerónimo to unleash his dogs. Inasmuch as the yellow mongrel's body had never been found, perhaps the creature was still alive. Maybe Doña Inés and Don Jerónimo made love that night but the really important event, the conception of Boy, occurred on another plane under the magical influence of Peta Ponce. As Mudito explains to Mother Benita,

Old women like Peta Ponce have the power to fold time over and confuse it, they multiply and divide it, events are refracted in their gnarled hands as

in the most brilliant prism, they cut the consecutive happening of things
into fragments they arrange in parallel form, they bend those fragments and
twist them into shapes that enable them to carry out their designs. (p. 181)

At the thought of having gone to bed with Doña Inés, Humberto
felt proud because the Peñalozas "were finally going to stop being
mere witnesses of beauty and were going to participate in it."
(p. 182) On the other hand, perhaps he did not actually have intercourse with Inés, but rather with Peta Ponce. It was dark and only
his sex organ touched the woman in the old servant's bed. Humberto ultimately convinces himself that although he and Peta Ponce
were excluded from the pleasure of love-making, it was their animal
vitality that actually conceived the child and made Doña Inés and
Don Jerónimo parents. Humberto's belief that Jerónimo stole his
fertility and that he (Humberto) deprived Jerónimo of his potency
further complicates the entire incident which concludes with Humberto's revelation that he fled to the Casa and disguised himself as a
deaf-mute in order to escape from the clutches of the lecherous Peta
Ponce.

Donoso's purpose in weaving this extraordinary skein of events, it
would seem, is to invalidate the traditional concepts of love by
uncovering the multiple layers of ambiguity composing the most
baffling of human emotions. Thus love emerges as a complex
mélange of ingredients including sexual desire, pleasure, and happiness; ambition, pride, and glory; possession, exploitation, and
humiliation; envy, rancor, fear, and vengeance; and superstition,
mystery, and magic.

The surrealistic revolt against reason in *The Obscene Bird of
Night* also finds expression through its depictions of the lack of unity
of the personality, one of the novel's major themes. Rejecting the
simplistic naturalistic view of man as a product of heredity and
environment, Donoso portrays the perpetual process of change in
his characters as evidenced by a complex series of fragmentations,
mutations, masks, and fusions of identities. The resulting kaleidoscopic glimpses of human consciousness reflect the frightening instability of the contemporary world in general and reinforce the author's conviction that the personality is nothing more than a collection of disguises.[14] Humberto, of course, represents the prime
example, his imagined symbiotic union with Jerónimo constituting
the mainspring that sets the entire chain of events in motion.

Moreover, the tension of opposites created by his alternating desire for power and extinction engender his evanescent identities that reflect his temporary states of mind. An analysis by one of the characters of the problems Humberto encountered as a writer while residing on La Rinconada recalls the surrealists' subjective approach to artistic creation and, at the same time, provides possible clues to the kind of fictional universe into which the author of the novel intends to immerse his readers:

Humberto had no talent for simplicity. He felt the need to twist normal things around, a kind of compulsion to take revenge and destroy, and he complicated and deformed his original project so much that it's as if he'd lost himself forever in the labyrinth he invented as he went along that was filled with darkness and terrors more real than himself and his other characters, always nebulous, fluctuating, never real human beings, always disguises, actors, dissolving greasepaint . . . yes, his obsessions and his hatreds were more important than the reality he needed to deny . . . (p. 392)

The fusion of Humberto's and Don Jerónimo's identities is balanced by a similar relationship between Peta Ponce and Doña Inés, although the antagonism between the male protagonists is entirely lacking in the case of their female counterparts. As a child, Doña Inés was saved from death by Peta Ponce who through witchcraft absorbed the girl's illness and pain into her own body, thus cementing their close association for life. Before Inés' marriage she introduces Jerónimo to her nursemaid and begs him to let the old woman live with them. The rationalistic Jerónimo, however, feels threatened by the enigmatic old woman, seeing in her the embodiment of the dark side of life that he has always so assiduously avoided. He secretly plans to get rid of her but on their wedding night Doña Inés refuses her body to him until he promises never for any reason to separate her from Peta Ponce. "From that night on, Jerónimo and Inés have never been alone in their marriage bed. Some shadow or other . . . always keeps them company." (p. 151) Many years later, when Doña Inés returns to the Casa from Europe, where she had an audience with the Pope and also sought medical treatment in a Swiss sanatorium, Mudito is convinced that the principal purpose of her journey was to have herself transformed into Peta Ponce. This she supposedly accomplished by undergoing a series of operations performed by the one-eyed Dr. Azula who had been Boy's personal physician on La Rinconada and somehow had

118 JOSÉ DONOSO

managed to obtain and preserve Peta Ponce's organs before moving his clinic to Switzerland. Thus, when Doña Inés is carried off to a mental hospital, Mudito joyfully imagines that he has been freed from his obsessive sexual desire for her and, simultaneously, from his fear of Peta Ponce. As shown below, Jerónimo is ultimately reabsorbed into Mudito's psyche, thus completing the symmetrical character schematization so typical of Donoso's works.[15]

Although the importance of symbols in the Chilean author's fiction has been discussed earlier, in *The Obscene Bird of Night* this literary ingredient acquires even greater significance.[16] Like the surrealists, Donoso utilizes symbolic images erupting from the unconscious as a means of creating a magical, autonomous reality destined to invade the objective realm and become an integral, luminous part of it. La Rinconada and the Casa are additional examples of the false home and family, a motif found in most of his works. Don Jerónimo and his four black dogs represent classical beauty, authority, and order which are threatened by mystery, chaos, and the grotesque embodied in the yellow bitch, Peta Ponce and Boy. This tension of opposites is also evident in the character of Iris Mateluna, the virgin harlot, as well as in the innocent, fairylike Doña Inés and the antithetical witch-goddess Peta Ponce.

Two vaguely interrelated symbols are the medallions that briefly illuminate the protagonist's imagination and the handkerchiefs given to Don Jerónimo by Peta Ponce. Like the medallions in *This Sunday*, these also seem to represent rigid socio-psychological categories formulated by rituals and imbedded in the minds of the characters. During his courtship of Doña Inés, Don Jerónimo views his future with his fiancée as a series of perfect medallions destined to last forever, but when she takes him to meet Peta Ponce in the old woman's dark, musty quarters, his reactions indicate his distrust and fear of another aspect of life, also symbolized by medallions, which he can neither understand nor accept.

The scene didn't fit into any medallion of eternal stone. And, if it did fit into any, it was into the other series, into the hostile legend that contradicted his own: the legend of the stained and the damned, who writhe on the left hand of God the Father Almighty. He had to pull Inés out of there immediately. To prevent her from taking part in this other series of medallions, the ones linked to servitude, to oblivion, to death. (p. 147)

Before they leave the old woman's lodgings, she gives Don Jerónimo three white exquisitely embroidered handkerchiefs which merely intensify his distrust of her because of their extraordinary beauty, the

> most perfect handkerchiefs he'd seen in his life . . . if he'd ever dreamed about handkerchiefs . . . he'd dreamed about . . . these . . . he held in his hands . . . that old woman introduced herself into his dreams and stole them. Otherwise, from where in the misery of her world, from what hidden source of power, could Peta have acquired the subtle sense of taste and the skill to make those three masterpieces? A searing pang of wonderment upset the neat order of his world as he recognized a powerful enemy in Peta Ponce. (p. 148)

This exquisitely made gift embodies the kind of beauty emanating from the dark, unconscious side of life which the surrealists believe has been stifled by the excessive rationalism they propose to undermine. After his marriage to Doña Inés, Don Jerónimo completely ignores Peta Ponce, but the old woman's and Humberto's magical roles in the conception of Boy resurrect the image of the medallions which emerge from Mudito's delirious psyche as symmetrically patterned symbols of an antiquated canon of values under threat of extinction by the forces of chaos.

> . . . Boy was going to be born . . . . Jerónimo had finally succeeded in taking Inés out of the static medallion of perfect marital happiness; his gallant hand was leading her toward their preordained positions in the next medallion, in which they'd appear as parents. While Peta and I, fantastic beings, grotesque monsters, carried out our mission of supporting that new medallion, holding it up straight from the outside, like a pair of magnificent heraldic animals. (p. 186)[17]

III *Existentialist Elements*

Although atheistic existentialism has much in common with surrealism,[18] its leading exponent, Jean-Paul Sartre, has generally rejected the Freudian and Jungian concepts of the unconscious as an escape from freedom and responsibility. Sartre reasons that if man can attribute his behavior to uncontrollable impulses arising from the unconscious, he is not the free, responsible creature existentialism proclaims him to be. Thus, the existentialists place little emphasis on automatic writing, nor do dreams and symbols play as important a role in their works as they do in surrealistic literature.

Humberto's vain search for meaning and absolutes in an unreasonable world illustrates the existentialist concept of the absurd[19] which is reinforced not only by the novel's ending but also by the episodes involving Boy and life on La Rinconada.[20] Having created this isolated realm of monsters as a bulwark of reason against anarchy, Don Jerónimo visits the estate many years later to announce his decision to terminate its existence and take his son back to the city. Boy's grotesque companions, however, proclaim their reluctance to leave their pleasant "papier mâché world" which they view as a kind of stage set, with themselves as "the props . . . the papier mâché heads, the masks." (pp. 394–95) Moreover, when Boy learns of his father's plan, he and the other monsters conspire to rid themselves of Don Jerónimo, declaring their unwillingness to be

his instruments or form part of a world he took it into his head to break up for no reason at all . . . like a minor god who never got past a frivolous and spoiled childhood in which his old toys always have to be replaced with new toys his boredom will make old and destroy . . . like an arteriosclerotic deity who, in creating the world, was stupid enough not to protect himself against the dangers that might arise in his creation. (pp. 395–96)

Mocked, pursued and treated like an outcast, Don Jerónimo dies a symbolic death which is discussed below. His creation and threatened destruction of La Rinconada for no reasonable purpose in some respects resembles Don Alejo's manipulation of Estación El Olivo in *Hell Has No Limits*. However, whereas Don Alejo is a corrupt, archaic god created by the town citizens for their own false sense of well-being, Don Jerónimo represents a modern god under siege by the monsters of reason he has created and cast adrift in a fragile world, highly vulnerable to the overpowering forces of irrationality.[21]

Donoso's characters often illustrate the existentialist psychology of Sartre whose theories on bad faith and the subject-object relationship between individuals help to explain his contention that conflict constitutes the basis for human associations.[22] In the case of Don Jerónimo and Humberto this conflict finds expression through a series of episodes reminiscent of the famous Sartrean "look" which converts the person seen into an object in the consciousness of the viewer-subject and gives rise to the constant interchange of sadistic

domination and masochistic dependency between the two characters. Humberto imagines that his own look objectifies Don Jerónimo
by controlling his (Jerónimo's) sexual potency. On the other hand,
Don Jerónimo believes that Humberto's look is filled with envy,
thus in a sense making Humberto an object of Don Jerónimo's
power. Moreover, Don Jerónimo's need to have Humberto watching him in order to be able to make love illustrates Sartre's theory of
the search for the unattainable being-in-itself-for-itself, that is, the
desire for permanence as a static object, which Humberto's look
confers on Don Jerónimo, and, at the same time, for freedom as a
dynamic subject, which Don Jerónimo achieves in his love-making.[23] Finally, Sartre's theories are also suggested by the portrayal
of Humberto, whose free, ever-evolving consciousness illustrates
the basic existentialist concept of man as a fluid succession of present selves in the process of determining his future essence, a process that ends only with death.

IV   *Time, Space and Aesthetic Unity*

In *The Obscene Bird of Night* Donoso depicts Humberto's unstable inner self through his interior monologues, a technique which
relates his works to those of the stream-of-consciousness novelists
such as James Joyce, William Faulkner, and Virginia Woolf, who
also penetrate the subliminal in order to reveal their characters'
psychic lives in spontaneous, uncensored thought patterns and symbolic images. This technique, so common in contemporary literature, gives the illusion of authorial disappearance, conveys dramatic
immediacy, and illustrates twentieth-century man's turn inward in
search of the truth that has eluded him through rationalistic
analysis. Usually somewhat difficult to comprehend, the stream-of-
consciousness novels present certain parallels with Henri Bergson's
philosophy, an understanding of which lends greater meaning and
coherence to this modern art form. Rejecting the concept of time as
a chronological entity that can be measured by the clock and arbi-
trarily divided into past, present, and future, Bergson stresses
psychological or subjective time (*la durée*) which he views as a con-
tinuous flow, often compared to a river, with past and present considered inseparable from memory and consciousness. He holds
great faith in intuition as a means of apprehending aesthetic experience and equates intuition with the novelist's imaginative ability to
immerse himself completely in his character's flow of consciousness,

seize his reality from within, and reproduce his rhythms of thought. Involuntary memory and free association emerge as major sources for the raw materials and dynamic psychic movement inherent in this type of fiction which seeks to capture thought in its inchoate stage and views reality as pulsating flux and perpetual change. For Bergson, personality is a process of ceaseless becoming, an inter-penetration of states of consciousness and fugitive sensory impres-sions caught in the inexorable flow of time. Similarly, experience is seen as a continual process of creative renewal filtered through an elastic and multidirectional temporal medium which, nevertheless, conveys the illusion of a dynamic and prolonged present. In view of the unstable reality in which stream-of-consciousness protagonists are portrayed, it is not surprising that they often assume more than a single identity through ephemeral disguises or mutations.

Several Bergsonian episodes in *The Obscene Bird of Night* are narrated by Mudito as he lies in a delirium directing his meandering thoughts to Mother Benita, the director of the Casa. In one of these passages the protagonist's identity crisis is intensified by his previ-ously mentioned longing for power and participation in life and, at the same time, by his terror of self-destruction which he feels would be brought about by communication with others. Thus, imprisoned in a world of his own making, he oscillates not only between delu-sions of omnipotence and impotence but, equally important here, between his imagined proliferation of identities and his temptation for self-annihilation in order to avoid the dangers of participation. This shuttling back and forth between extremes, so typical of the schizophrenic mind, produces the kaleidoscopic patterns erupting from Mudito's psyche as he recreates or imagines several incidents out of his past.

One six-page interior monologue begins with his terror of being brutalized by the police, his pleas to Mother Benita for protection, and his fancied self-inflicted wounds in order to reverse the relation-ship between himself and his pursuers. "Wounded like this, I'm safe, because now they're the ones who are afraid of me, not I of them . . ." (p. 117) Mudito then describes how he stole one of the one hundred copies of his book of poems from the library of Don Jerónimo who had bought them to help launch the young writer's career. He took only one copy because, upon entering Don Jerónimo's home, he was seized by an irrational fear of destruction:

". . . as I stood on a rug of such deep tones . . . I was paralyzed by the terror
of drowning in them and being swallowed up by their elegance. . . . How
could I help fearing that the rug resonant with symbols would suck me
under . . ." (p. 118)

Humberto's recollection that both Jerónimo's and Inés' names
appear on every page of his book evokes poetic visions of the
couple's enviable, idyllic existence and leads him to calculate that as
author of the volume his own name appears a total of 9,300 times in
the one hundred copies. His promise to read his poems some day to
Mother Benita unleashes his satirical remarks on the vapid criticism
and the superficial themes sometimes typical of Modernism, the
literary movement that probably influenced him.[24]

I'll read a passage here and there of the flashy prose, of the naive fancies, of
that consummate writer with the ultra-artistic style, with such choice sensi-
bility, that budding poet of lyrics redolent of spring, that talented man just
emerging from his chrysalis to breathe in the fragrant air of a rosy future
that will add honor to the literature of his country, and, after reading you
one of those portraits of women I used to write then, because I didn't know
any and could only imagine them sheathed in a wave of Oriental perfumes,
because perfumes were always Oriental in those days, and tunics always
sumptuously embroidered, and poses languid, and those cruel but smiling
flirts always broke men's hearts, and there was always a full moon . . .
(pp. 118–19)

This world of poetic perfection evokes two recurring symbols of
omnipotence and idealism—a monstrous papier-mâché head and a
Swiss chalet—before Mudito's fluctuating psyche returns to the
theft of his book and his terrifying escape from Don Jerónimo's
house with the police in hot pursuit. Immediately thereafter his
impulse to burn all his books and papers in order to erase his identity, and thus suppress his feelings of vulnerability, produces the
visual motif that foreshadows the novel's final scene: "I'll throw
them from this black steel bridge to the rocky riverbed and, after
letting myself down here, I'll light a sheet of paper, two, maybe a
notebook, to warm my hands a little because it will be cold." (p. 120)
The blaze attracts a circle of faceless people wearing disguises and
waiting for Mudito to join them as soon as his identity is obliterated.
The grotesque leitmotif of a "knot of children and flea-bitten dogs on

the ground" forming "a single monstrous animal" (p. 121) serves to underscore the protagonist's disintegrating world, a theme which finds renewed expression in the vanishing disguises of the faceless:

> . . . the pallor of their filth, the grays of their sumptuous tatters . . . the shininess of the coat of mail . . . emblems that are patches . . . princes with their courts of dwarfs. . . . Take off their disguises and they're reduced to people like me, without faces or features, who have to go rummaging in trash cans . . . in order to put together one disguise one day, another disguise the next, in order to give themselves an identity. . . . (p. 121)

For Mudito this nightmarish masquerade evokes both the oft-repeated phrase of his father, "to be someone, Humberto, that's the important thing," and his sister's pose in imitation of a postcard photograph because "her own face wasn't enough." (p. 122) The tempo of the monologue quickens with the protagonist's increased awareness of the "mobility" and "fluid existence" of his ever-changing masks which enable him to evade his oppressive self and offer him a measure of omnipotence, "the freedom of never being the same . . . today I'm myself and tomorrow no one can find me, not even I myself, because you're what you are only for as long as the disguise lasts." (p. 122) He then imagines himself joining the faceless masses around the fire and losing his identity forever because "that's the only way I'll be able to free myself from Don Jerónimo . . . and from Peta Ponce. . . ." (p. 123) However, the thought of the remaining copies of his book in Don Jerónimo's library and of "things I preserve and can't relinquish yet" (p. 123) rekindles his lust for power and prevents his withdrawal. His stream of consciousness ends just as it began, with his terror of the police and his pleas to Mother Benita to save him.

The intuitive eruptions of visual reality and thematic obsessions set forth in the previous passage attest to the author's creative imagination and illustrate the Bergsonian concept of time (*la durée*) as a series of fluid, interlocking psychic states mutually penetrating one another. Also demonstrated by Humberto's monologue, as well as by virtually all stream-of-consciousness fiction, is the Bergsonian theory that time acquires true meaning and significance only through a medium of sensory experience provided by an individual observer. It follows then that the temporal realm in this type of literature is viewed, not linearly through the mind of a traditional, omniscient narrator, but rather from an infinite number of spatial perspectives, each having its own validity and no single perspective encompassing a total vision of reality. Modern technology and psychology have also altered traditional time and space concepts by making man aware of primitive and advanced cultures existing side by side simultaneously and by exploring the world of dreams where temporal and spatial boundaries blur or completely disappear.

As a result of these philosophical, psychological, and technological advances, the notion of time has tended to become spatialized or fused with that of space. Furthermore, the traditional emphasis on linear plot, carefully set forth themes and analytical character development has been abandoned by many novelists who utilize structural principles such as the random juxtaposition of fragmentary reality in order to disrupt or abolish chronology, minimize causality, and thus delineate a composite fictional universe more attuned to the world of today. The resulting montage of conflicting temporal and spatial relationships conveys the illusion of dynamic movement and captures the simultaneity of rapidly occurring events that envelop and bewilder contemporary existential man.

Generally speaking the preceding remarks apply to *The Obscene Bird of Night*, which is likely to strike the casual reader as an extremely confusing, diffuse novel, haphazard in its stylistic composition, jagged in its structural design, and utterly lacking in symmetry. And indeed, as an anti-novel, it was more than likely intended to create an initial impression of chaos and ambiguity in order to jolt the reader onto new planes of awareness. However, a serious look at the work reveals an artistically conceived fictional universe enclosed in a carefully outlined framework into which meaning and coherence have been injected by a wide variety of unifying elements. First of all, the narrative point of view is not multiple, as one is initially led to suspect, but rather comprises a single perspective, that of the protagonist whose haunting, distorted interpretation of reality provides a remarkable intensity of focus encompassing a compact, self-contained world. Humberto's proliferation of identities explains the various narrative voices: his own, Don Jerónimo's and, most important of all, Mudito's. Moreover, the biography of Don Jerónimo, the birth of Boy and most of the episodes on La Rinconada involving the monsters constitute sections of Humberto's book, which explains the third-person point of view in these passages. And the fact that Mudito's character is pat-

terned after Teiresias, the great seer of Thebes in Greek mythology[25] explains his uncanny knowledge of everything that occurs in
the Casa as well as his mysterious insight into the actions and moti-
vations of the other characters.

In *The Obscene Bird of Night* chronological time has been virtually obliterated by the interior monologues and abrupt dislocations
between chapters and scenes. Nevertheless, clues have been provided to help the reader rearrange the scrambled events within a
clearly defined temporal frame. The central action of the novel occurs in approximately one year, starting with Brígida's funeral in
the Casa, when Misiá Raquel promises to send the old women a gift
from her farm in memory of the deceased, and terminating with the
arrival of the five hundred pumpkins, the delivery of which, we are
told, is delayed by a little more than a year. This brief span of time
elapses during the 1960's, a fact made evident by references to news
stories such as the Vietnamese War, Fidel Castro's sugar harvest,
the Hippy Revolution and Salvador Allende's political campaign.[26]

One of the novel's two principal flashbacks occurs in the late
eighteenth century when the Casa was built, and the other during
World War I when Don Jerónimo returns from Europe at the age of
thirty-one.[27] His marriage to his young bride, Doña Inés, soon
thereafter, is followed by the birth of Boy six years later. The
episodes that take place subsequently on La Rinconada last approximately fifteen years at which time Dr. Azula supposedly per-
forms brain surgery on Boy and moves to Switzerland. Finally, Doña
Inés' organ transplants in Dr. Azula's clinic at sixty-three years of
age and her return to the Casa just before its demolition once again
suggest the decade of the 1960's.[28]

It should be made clear, however, that space, not time, plays the
dominant role in the novel's structural organization. Indeed, because the two major settings, La Rinconada and the Casa,[29] represent diametrical opposites frequently confused within the protagonist's mind, dynamic movement in a sense tends to abolish
time, creating the impression of an eternal, dreamlike present between two fundamental spatial entities. The novel consists of thirty
chapters, the first nine (part I) dealing principally with events occurring in the Casa, the following nine (part II) taking place mostly on
La Rinconada, and the last twelve (part III) alternating between the
two settings and depicting their common disintegration. Each of the
three parts climaxes with a major crisis in the protagonist's illness,

the first of which involves the previously discussed burning of his papers; the end of part II describes his ulcer operation and subsequent move from La Rinconada to the Casa; the final pages of the book dramatize his disappearance.

An outsider in both of the novel's major settings, the narrator shuttles from one extreme to the other in his frantic search for omnipotence and oblivion. On La Rinconada his aspirations of achieving fame as a writer and power as Don Jerónimo's representative are thwarted by his feelings of claustrophobia and his paranoiac fears of the jeering monsters which provoke his ulcer attack. In the Casa he is the only male in a matriarchal society of superstitious old women whose irrational behavior borders on anarchy. In this chaotic environment Mudito not only attains omnipotence and nothingness through his multiple identities and ultimate annihilation, but also through the proliferation of patios and corridors, which symbolize freedom and imagination, and through his obsessive efforts to return to a womblike enclosure by covering up doors, windows, and passageways.

Humberto's shift of consciousness from La Rinconada to the Casa at the end of part II is a masterfully written passage that conveys his mental aberrations during or immediately following his ulcer operation. Addressing Mother Benita in an interior monologue, Mudito recalls a feeling of timelessness, his escape from Don Jerónimo's estate with twenty per cent of his organs, and his life as a begger roaming the streets in destitution but relieved at the thought that Peta Ponce is no longer pursuing him with her lecherous intentions. Suddenly his mind glides back to La Rinconada where Mother Benita is replaced at his bedside by the dwarf monster Emperatriz who, dressed in her wedding gown, is waiting to marry Mudito at the first opportunity. When he tries to rape her she runs away, abandoning him in a basement room with a false window and no exits. Threatened by extinction, he scratches and claws to find his way out but only uncovers layers of newspapers full of tragic headlines of famines, floods and earthquakes. And then ". . . there's no more paper now, there's mud, a dungeon where I was locked up in the center of the earth and sealed off. . . ." (p. 235) He continues to dig, hoping to "create patios and rooms to move about in" (p. 236) but finds breathing more and more difficult in a steadily shrinking space. Images appear before him of orange trees, light, and water in which he imagines himself to be swimming, and then all at once he becomes aware of voices from the Casa already familiar to the reader:

> . . . we must sweep up the rubble from this wall and leave everything clean, ripped old newspapers . . . sweep everything, Mudito, pile it into a neat little heap so there won't be any filth around . . . all the leftist newspapers do is attack her [Doña Inés] and make her look ridiculous because the beatification fell through. How foolish, all the millions she has and she takes the vow of poverty! I'm sure it's to get even with Jerónimo because he signed the Casa away without consulting her . . . and when she gets here she'll find that the Casa's been sold at auction . . ." (pp. 236–37)

A number of striking parallels between the legend of the Casa's origin and the four leading characters contribute to the novel's extraordinary compositional balance by creating a magical impression of cyclical recurrence. According to the legend, when the girl-saint and her nursemaid were suspected of witchcraft, the girl's father entered her room and, finding himself confronted with some untold horror, raised his poncho to prevent his sons from witnessing the spectacle. Immediately thereafter he sent his daughter to spend the rest of her days in a convent destined to be known as the Casa. The story of how she saved the edifice during an earthquake by forming a cross with her arms and gnarled hands, like those of her old companion, made her a saint in the eyes of her family. However, the peasants in the region preferred the tale of the girl-witch and her nursemaid who were identified respectively with a *chonchón*, an ugly bird of ill omen, and a mongrel yellow dog, which haunted the countryside by night under a full moon. In her long conversations with Doña Inés, Peta Ponce combines both versions of the story, but Mudito theorizes that Don Jerónimo managed to make his wife forget the tale of the girl-witch. "Don Jerónimo must have raised his poncho to cover Inés for the very definite purpose of separating that portion of the family secret he could control, the story of the girl-saint, from the terrifying shadows of the popular legend . . ." (p. 285) This action by Don Jerónimo has the effect of suppressing Doña Inés' instinctual nature, arousing in her the fear of extinction and, because she cannot give birth to a normal son, causing her to seek the beatification of the girl-saint in order to assure for herself a role in the family legend.

Here the narrator-protagonist injects another note of ambiguity by speculating that Peta Ponce, rather than Doña Inés, is a descendant of the girl-saint who was more than likely whisked off to the convent because she was made pregnant by a farm hand introduced into her bedroom by her nursemaid. The illegitimate child, presumably raised on the estate as a foundling, was Peta Ponce's ancestor. Mudito feels certain that the reason he thought he made love to Doña Inés that night on La Rinconada was because Peta Ponce, with whom he is now convinced he actually had intercourse, bore faint vestiges of the girl-saint, "although generations and generations of humiliated forebears have buried all trace of noble blood in the depths of her half-breed witch's face." (p. 289) Thus, in the protagonist's mind the crafty old servant comes to embody both the legendary girl-witch and the blessed girl-saint.

In spite of the pervasive uncertainty created by Mudito's delirium, the parallels between the legend and the novel's central plot are numerous and obvious. In each a deliberate attempt is made to establish a dichotomy between the tales of the witch and the saint, that is, to suppress the dark, underside of human existence which poses a threat to the privileged and supposedly more rational elements in control of society. Nevertheless, the identities of the two Inés de Azcoitías fuse with those of their old nursemaids, both of whom play key roles in the procreation of their charges' offspring. However, whereas the Blessed Inés of the legend is believed to have saved the convent from destruction and died "in the odor of sanctity," Doña Inés is overwhelmed by the mysterious forces embodied in Peta Ponce, fails in her efforts to preserve the Casa from demolition and probably ends her life in an insane asylum. Her tragic fate conveys a theme recurring throughout Donoso's works, i.e., that the rational side of human nature is no match for the overpowering passions engendered by the social injustice and suppressed instincts so characteristic of today's world.

La Rinconada and the Casa are frequently linked by parallels and identity fusions which, though tending to balance and unify the two juxtaposed settings, create additional elements of ambiguity. For example, it is suggested on several occasions that Iris Mateluna's miraculous baby has been begotten by Don Jerónimo with the aid of Mudito's envious eyes, and that the long-awaited child will provide the only chance Jerónimo has "of being great and noble again, by meeting the challenge of being father to a monster son." (pp. 109–10) A vague spiritual kinship between Boy and Iris' unborn infant is also established by the fact that, just as Peta Ponce's magical

intervention brought about the conception of Don Jerónimo's monstrous offspring, the image of Iris' child is seen rising from the vapor
of María Benítez' pot of saltwort infusion.[30] And toward the end of
the novel, when Iris finally gives birth to Mudito, the latter's identity is linked to Boy's by the words of one of the old women:

> What a skinny, puny baby you had, Iris, a child with such sad-looking eyes!
> But it's the child. There's no doubt about that. It's the child, it's Boy, look,
> why he seems to have a tiny little halo but still and all a halo . . ." (p. 359)

Even more significant are the identity fusions that prepare the
denouement. Because Don Jerónimo wishes to put an end to both
the Casa and La Rinconada, Mudito and Boy consider him a grave
threat and express their desires to do away with him. Thus, after
Doña Inés is taken to a mental institution, Mudito walls up the
doors and windows of the Casa to prevent Don Jerónimo from entering[31] and then leaves through the only remaining exit. At this
same time Boy escapes from La Rinconada for a period of five days
after which he returns and awaits Jerónimo's visit to the estate. As
mentioned above, Jerónimo is scorned by the monsters who deliberately scoff at him in order to make him feel like the only abnormal
person among them, just as Humberto had been led to believe of
himself. Jerónimo gradually loses his rational awareness and is reabsorbed into Humberto's (Mudito's) psyche while, in his (Jerónimo's)
disturbed state of mind, La Rinconada is transformed into the Casa:

> . . . he was weary, he'd suddenly grown weary of all this, it wasn't com-
> forting to have them laugh at his advanced years, to make him walk on all
> fours, to order him to wash windows, sweep hallways and empty rooms and
> galleries and interminable courts, to seal off doors, plaster walls, burn old
> newspapers . . . (pp. 402–403)

Jerónimo had been invited to Emperatriz's yearly costume ball
but the monsters had intentionally misinformed him, telling him the
theme would be the Court of Miracles, which in reality was the
motif of the previous year when La Rinconada was decorated like
the Casa. Now he suddenly finds himself at the ball, first naked and
then in tatters in the midst of the other guests, all garbed in exotic
elegance. Insulted by his appearance, they drag him to a pond and
force him to look at his reflection while somebody tosses a rock into
the water, shattering his image. Horrified at his facial distortions, he

attempts to remove what he believes to be a mask and then begins
to search for his clothing in an imagined labyrinthian structure, the
doors of which have been sealed shut.[32] Finally he returns to the
pond where he drowns while trying once again to tear the ugly mask
off his face.[33] Several hours later the monsters discover his body and
send it to the capital where, as a former senator, Jerónimo is given a
state funeral.[34] Meanwhile Boy has requested that Dr. Azula perform an operation on his brain regardless of the consequences in
order to destroy all memory of his father and of the five days he
spent outside La Rinconada. The doctor's reply predicts Boy's fate.

If I did it, I'd also have to cut out a large part of your brain, and then, of
course, you'd have the mere shadow of consciousness left, you'd live in a
kind of twilight, in a limbo not very different from death without sinking
into it, alive, but . . ." (p. 401)

   With Don Jerónimo's reabsorption into Mudito's psyche and
Boy's imminent descent into a kind of twilight zone or limbo, only
Mudito's destiny remains undetermined. Throughout the novel repeated references are made to the *imbunche* myth which is closely
related to the narrator's schizophrenic yearnings as well as to the
sequence of events leading to his ultimate enclosure in several
layers of sacks. On one occasion he expresses his desire to become
an *imbunche* so that his eyes will be sewn shut and he will thus
render Jerónimo impotent forever. On the other hand, Humberto
feels imprisoned on La Rinconada, as if he were in "a sealed world,
stifling, like living inside a sack and trying to bite through the burlap
to get out or let in the air and find out if your destiny lies outside or
inside or somewhere else . . ." (p. 199) On occasions the *imbunche*
represents a means of protection as illustrated by Mudito's sealing
off the doors and windows of the Casa in order to keep out Jerónimo
and make the old edifice an "*imbunche* Casa, all of us old women
being *imbunches* now, we fear nothing." (p. 379) When Mudito
becomes Iris' miraculous baby and the instrument of salvation for
the elderly women, his antithetical helplessness and dominion are
increasingly evident. Pampered, worshipped, and completely
dominated by them, he is wrapped in sacks which isolate him from
evil and thus permit him to take them to heaven. Nevertheless, in
spite of his inability to see, hear, speak or breathe, he feels secure,
independent, and contented as the crones "address their supplica-

tions to me, prostrate, imploring me because they know that I'm powerful now that I'm finally going to perform the miracle." (p. 423)

In the last chapter the outcome of Mudito's dilemma is interrupted by a series of hilarious events occurring in the Casa. The buses arrive with four priests eager to take the occupants to the new home provided for them by Brígida's estate.[35] However, the orderly procedure of departure planned by Father Azócar is completely disrupted by the anarchic old ladies' disagreement over Brígida's family name and the delivery of the above-mentioned pumpkins, an "invasion of creatures from another geological age . . . whose growing number couldn't be stopped . . ." (p. 431)

When the buses leave, Mudito finds himself abandoned in the Casa, still bound tightly in burlap sacks. Sexless, blissfully content to exist in a kind of timeless, brightly illuminated limbo, asphyxiating and wracked with pain, terrified of death and desperately wanting to emerge from his obscure, cocoon-like existence, he ponders over the imminent destruction of his labyrinthian world of adobe which will return to its natural state of level ground.[36] Upon hearing somebody stirring in a corner nearby, he attempts to bite through the cloth in order to communicate with the unknown person. However, whenever he manages to break through the last layer of sacking "in order to be born or die" (p. 435), a gnarled hand sews up the opening. The chewing and mending continue for centuries until "there are no more orifices." (p. 436) Now converted into something similar to an *imbunche,* Mudito is tossed into a trash bag which an old woman slowly carries through the jungle of pumpkin runners and foliage enveloping the cloister. Hundreds of years later she exits onto the street, crosses brightly lighted avenues and makes her way to the bank of a river under a bridge where a group of hags hover around a dying fire. When the others depart, she empties the contents of her bundle on the fire in order to revive the flames and briefly ward off the chill of the night air.

In a few minutes, there's nothing left under the bridge. Only the black smudge the fire left on the stones, and a blackish tin can with a wire handle. The wind overturns it and it rolls over the rocks and falls into the river. (p. 438)

This description of Mudito's end typifies the entire novel for its symbolic imagery and pervasive ambiguity. Donoso himself refuses to accept any one interpretation of his protagonist's confinement but acknowledges that it could signify birth, death, castration, masochistic self-destruction, the Freudian womb-security concept, the return to the inchoate world of the uroboros, the schizophrenic desire for and fear of self-fulfillment and ruination, the disastrous result of domination and injustice, alienated man's frustrating search for communication, the existentialists' vain pursuit of Being-in-itself-for-itself, or the point of perfect freedom and harmony the surrealists set as the goal for their creative endeavor.[37] Almost equally ambiguous are the pumpkins which constitute an element of the absurd and also suggest rebirth and primeval savagery with their fabulous fertility and "hard gray shell, rugged like a prehistoric animal's." (p. 430) And although Mudito's annihilation in the bonfire under the bridge would seem to represent the ultimate in finality, the river image immediately following evokes perpetual movement and cyclical renewal.

The erratic meanderings of Humberto Peñaloza's mind acquire coherence not only through the unities of time, place and narrative voice, but also through the obsessive repetition of symbols, motifs, phrases, and themes which lend pattern and rhythm to an obscure private world. Although some recurring images have been alluded to above in connection with surrealism, additional evidence of the novel's artistic form and textural density is provided by the following symbolic elements, most of which emerge from the anarchic minds of Mudito or the old women in the Casa. A leitmotif evoking pathetic loneliness is Clemencia's most prized possession, a lock of hair from Rafaelito, the son of her former employer. The madness of old age is illustrated by Amalia's perpetual search for a lost finger, while the broken statues stored in the Casa reflect the fractured, deteriorating personalities of its inhabitants. The old women's obsession with the miraculous baby represents their hopes for salvation,[38] but their effort to isolate the child from the outside world and their neatly tied packages stored under their beds demonstrate their bid to keep a lingering hold on life through domination and possession. Their desire for power is also demonstrated by their envious references to Brígida's elaborate funeral which they mistakenly believe was paid for by her grateful employers.

One of many symbols of destitution is the brown coat Iris Mateluna receives from Brígida to conceal her pregnancy and then loses to Doña Inés in the dog-racing game. Just as Mudito's Swiss chalet represents the unattainable ideal home, the Children's Village slated to be erected on the site of the demolished Casa emerges as a kind of El Dorado hoax, and the giant papier-mâché head as a symbol of ephemeral glory and delight. The search for delight also finds expression in the dog-racing and telephone games played in the Casa, but whereas the former underscores man's efforts to circumscribe his universe in order to control his destiny, the latter reiterates the fusion-of-identities theme. The yellow bitch and her moon accomplice inject an element of fate into the characters' lives, and the *chonchón*, the ugly winged creature of ill omen, is a mythical counterpart of the obscene bird in the novel's title.[39]

Although the projected destruction of the Casa is a frequent topic of conversation among its inhabitants, a symbolic event in chapter nineteen seems to precipitate the structure's rapid decline. This entire unit takes place in the chapel where Mother Benita and Mudito witness the theft of the Eucharist lamp by Father Azócar who, unaware that he is being observed, stands on a wobbly chair to reach the valuable object and utters a curse when he stumbles and falls.[40] The subsequent moral decay becomes apparent when the abandoned inhabitants of the Casa send Iris into the streets to practice prostitution and, desperate for food, begin to assault passersby and rob stores in the neighborhood. The actual demolition of the edifice is cloaked in the ambiguity of Mudito's last interior monologue which first projects its fall and then, centuries later, describes the old woman's departure through the front door with Mudito in her trash bag.

The novel's impressive array of styles and techniques reflects not only the author's profound aesthetic preoccupations but also his protagonist's various levels of consciousness. The naïve, stereotyped language characteristic of fairy tales conveys the story of the Casa's legendary origin: "Once upon a time, years and years ago, there was a landowner, very rich but kindhearted too, who owned vast tracts of land in every part of the country. . . ." (p. 23) The highly visual descriptions of the elaborate ball held on La Rinconada are set forth in mannered, decorative prose reminiscent of an ornate baroque painting.

Familiar and unfamiliar faces are dancing in the light, with monumental wigs like tall frosted pastry, with golden turbans and strands of pearls, opalescent masks, brocaded dominoes, pointed satin slippers dancing a minuet, whirling crinolines, three-cornered hats in hand . . . beautiful

papier-mâché masks . . . the couples are dancing, fingers touching deli-
cately, they're drinking from chilled glasses. . ." (p. 406)

The passages relating Jerónimo's youth, life as a senator, and the
birth of his son are related by an omniscient narrator, a traditional,
rationalistic technique typifying the well-made nineteenth-century
novel and used here to mirror the conservative bourgeois society
depicted.[41] The episodes involving the monsters on La Rinconada
constitute a Kafkaesque view of the world characterized by grotesque distortions but presented in a precise and disciplined literary
style. The vernacular of lower-class youths concerned primarily with
sex, popular music, and comic books is the linguistic vehicle for the
dialogues overheard by Mudito on the street outside the Casa and in
the magazine shop nearby. Perhaps most important, however, are
Mudito's interior monologues in which the temporal and spatial
dislocations, the scrambled point of view, and the violation of classical syntax denote the destruction of traditional form that typifies
much twentieth-century fiction and reflects the novel's central
theme of disintegration. These monologues also reflect the unstable
psyche of the protagonist whose graphic, dreamlike transpositions of
reality occasionally suggest the author's affinity with the surrealist
painters. In the following exemplary passage Mudito is fearfully
accompanying Mother Benita to the recently deceased Brígida's
room for the purpose of disposing of her belongings. Their walk
through the empty, crumbling structure evokes a kind of nightmarish descent into the unconscious projected here as a mysterious
realm of muffled sounds and foreboding that lies beyond logic and,
at the same time, rejects the stale accumulations of the past.
Moreover, the implications of man alone in a shadowy, remote atmosphere convey the absurdity of life and the dreadful metaphysical
void captured on the canvases of the Italian surrealistic painter
Giorgio di Chirico, a favorite of Donoso.[42]

Watch out for that step, Mother, it's a step, not a shadow, and we come out
into still another court that's not the one where Brígida lived, so we have to
go down other passageways . . . One, then a second empty room, rows of
vacant rooms, more doors . . . more rooms to cross, shattered window-
panes coated with dust, the semidarkness sticking to the dried-up
walls . . . Another court . . . the court with the palm tree, the one with
the linden . . . the refectory court no one uses . . . endless courts and
cloisters connected by corridors that never end. . . . Watch out,

Mother . . . let's step around this rubble, better walk down this corridor
that leads into still another court that's on a different level because of the
now-forgotten purposes it once served, and opens onto rooms where sounds
are softened by cobwebs and on to galleries where the echoes of forgotten
comings and goings linger. . . ." (pp. 13–14)

V Conclusions

The Obscene Bird of Night presents a surrealistic metaphor of
human existence that affords its reader a wider range of awareness
and understanding by compelling him to abandon the realm of logic
in order to participate in a phantasmagorical world of paradox and
ambiguity. The book sets forth no theses and resolves no issues.
Rather, it conveys an absurd, unstable reality without absolutes in
which man appears doomed to suffer terror, death, and nothingness. Donoso reveals most of the pessimistic elements of existentialism but refuses to accept this philosophy's more positive tenets of
responsibility, human solidarity, and commitment to one's ideals.
His pessimism is further underscored by his protagonists' lack of
love and feelings of isolation from which they attempt to escape
through self-evasion in the form of domination, submission, or conformity. The resulting loss of self and fragmentation of the personality effect disguises, mutations, and the fusion of identities, as demonstrated in the cases of Humberto-Don Jerónimo-Boy-Mudito
and Doña Inés-Peta Ponce. These important aspects of Donoso's
psychology illustrate his repeatedly expressed denial of the unity of
the personality and help to explain why his characters emerge as
frustrated, masked antiheroes often acting out roles imposed on
them by others.

Due to its formal complexity, perplexing thematic possibilities
and broad tonal range, *The Obscene Bird of Night* is the type of work
scholars are likely to analyze and puzzle over for years to come. Its
protean view of today's world is ironic, tragic, philosophically profound and psychologically penetrating. Donoso's blend of logic with
absurdity and of objective reality with imagination conveys an ambivalent view of man trapped in a topsy-turvy environment in which
values are visibly crumbling. Indeed, reason and rationalism, which
have been so highly acclaimed by modern man, resemble ephemeral flashes of light emerging from, and being submerged by, the
overwhelmingly powerful instinctual forces comprising the mysterious underside of existence. Thus Jerónimo, the rational element of

Humberto's personality, is drawn into the latter's unconscious which is represented by both Boy and Mudito, and Doña Inés in a sense loses her identity to Peta Ponce, the witch-goddess who, it is playfully suggested, may turn out to be the sole survivor.[43] The author imposes a measure of order and logic on chaos by means of a wide variety of unifying devices which create an aesthetic essence discernible only to the sophisticated reader willing to participate actively in discovering the intricate designs so ingeniously woven into the fictional framework. Brilliant, baffling and haunting, *The Obscene Bird of Night* unquestionably protests against existing conditions in the contemporary world, but, far more significantly, the book achieves new levels of contact with reality by probing, scrutinizing, and extolling, as only art can do, the mysterious, uncharted depths of the human psyche. For this reason, it can be described as a monumental, masterfully orchestrated tribute to consciousness.

CHAPTER 6

Sacred Families:
Middle-Class Reality and Fantasy

I   *Plots and Themes*

A FTER total immersion in the phantasmagorical world of *The Obscene Bird of Night*, one is likely to find Donoso's latest fictional endeavor somewhat anticlimactic. *Tres novelitas burguesas (Sacred Families)*, 1973, is characterized by a return to a more traditional structural technique, a reworking of some of Donoso's well-known obsessions and the continued reliance on symbols to illuminate his fictional universe. Still, these short novels not only initiate an incursion into a realm of humor and fantasy unlike anything seen heretofore in the author's works, but also reflect the two years of his residency in Barcelona (1969–71), the setting of all three pieces. A measure of unity is achieved through the reappearance of the same characters, the most important of whom are three couples about forty years of age belonging to Spain's professional, upper-middle class. Although the vanity and superficiality of this milieu are satirized, the themes of social injustice and decay underlying the previous novels have been virtually abandoned. Rather, the emphasis here is on the complexity of human relations, the vain search for identity, and the subtle creation of setting and atmosphere.

Sacred Families sets forth three basic themes, all of which also figure prominently in the earlier works: the conflict between order and chaos, the instability of the personality, and the dialectical interplay of domination and dependence—or spoliation and submission —evidenced by the characters. A spoof on women's liberation, "Chatanooga ChooChoo" (Chattanooga Choo-Choo) presents a fantastic series of events affecting the lives of two couples: Dr. Anselmo Prieto and his wife Magdalena, and architect Ramón del Solar and

138

his mistress, a famous model named Sylvia Corday. Sylvia allows herself to be dismembered and reassembled by Ramón whom she in turn manages to dominate by utilizing her shifting identities or masks to give him the illusion of constantly initiating a new affair. Her domination of her lover takes the form of periodically removing and replacing his genitals. Sylvia first meets Magdalena at a party where, dressed identically in the style of the 1940's, they sing "The Chattanooga Choo-Choo," accompanying their number with perfectly coordinated, wooden gyrations similar to those of the Andrew Sisters. Having detected in Magdalena a kindred spirit, Sylvia has a brief affair with Anselmo, whom she manipulates just as she has Ramón, and then communicates to Magdalena her ability to control members of the opposite sex. The two women join forces in order to exercise their power over their male adversaries, evoking from Anselmo the following reflections: ". . . to use us, yes, that's what they want, that's why they put on an act of submission, and when a man submits to their charms, the first thing they do is take away his virility."[1] He also suspects that when women meet in cafés to chat and drink coffee, their real purpose is to intrigue and exchange ideas on how to wield power over their husbands and lovers.

Anselmo's dream sequence, which begins while his wife is massaging his back, brings the story to its conclusion. Magdalena's nimble fingers gradually dismember his body and pack it neatly into a suitcase which she takes to a party she and Sylvia have agreed to attend. She also carries a mysterious package given to her by Sylvia after the latter's brief affair with Anselmo. When Sylvia arrives with Ramón's body, also dismantled, she tells Magdalena, ". . . that package I gave you, do you remember? I made a mistake . . . you have Ramón's and I have Anselmo's." (p. 95) Amused and not in the least disconcerted, the two women proceed to assemble their mates, dress them in identical green corduroy suits and then make them perform "The Chattanooga Choo-Choo." In the final scene of reconciliation Magdalena restores the repentant Anselmo's missing parts, and a fragile though welcome truce between them ensues.

"Átomo verde número cinco" (Green Atom Number Five) describes the disintegrating psychic world of Roberto and Marta Ferrer, a well-to-do, childless couple, after their move to a new apartment they have decorated in the most exquisite taste. An empty room in the flat that Roberto refuses to furnish until he feels inspired to do so symbolizes the void in their lives which they have always believed could be filled with the purchase of material things,". . . beloved objects that serve as bridges for communication or as masks that would protect them from hostile nakedness. . . ." (p. 172) An amateur painter in addition to being a dentist, Roberto has recently given his most cherished picture, Green Atom Number Five, to his wife on their fifteenth wedding anniversary because she requested it instead of the emerald he had planned to buy her. The disappearance of this painting, a symbol of stability in their lives, precipitates the deterioration of their relationship by unleashing a series of disputes regarding its value, Roberto's merit as an artist, and Marta's inability to bear children. Marta is also obliged to admit she requested the painting not because she preferred it to jewelry, but rather out of pity for her husband. "You were feeling so low, so depressed, remember how you get when all you do is repeat that nothing makes sense, that all we do is buy things . . . ." (p. 125)

From this moment on, objects either vanish mysteriously from the couple's lodgings or are taken away under their very eyes by friends or strangers. After Marta becomes involved in a minor accident while attempting to stop a truck carrying off a piece of their furniture, she and her husband lock themselves in their apartment in order to preserve their remaining possessions. Their bitterness and resentment steadily mount, generating an atmosphere of suspicion in which they blame one another for all their misfortunes. After so many years together, moreover, each begins to feel the other has invaded his privacy, divesting him of everything from personal effects to individual identity. The appearance of a slip of paper in Roberto's desk bearing the title of the missing picture and an unknown address induces them to take a taxi to a warehouse district of the city where they lose their way in a maze of narrow streets. Increasingly distraught over their lost painting, they become involved in a violent quarrel with the taxi driver, rob him of his belongings and then suddenly turn on each other with harsh accusations and insults. In a final paroxysm of hate they tear each other's clothes off, each insanely grasping for the other's possessions and then, naked and horror struck, back off "like two animals that separate at the precise moment before attacking in order to destroy or possess one another, or before turning around to flee, howling with terror until they become lost in the vast, empty landscape." (pp. 187–88)

The central figure of "Gaspard de la nuit" ("Gaspard de la Nuit"), the best of the three novelettes, is a sixteen-year-old boy named Mauricio who arrives from Madrid to spend the summer in Barcelona with his divorced mother Sylvia Corday, the model and mistress of Ramón del Solar in Chattanooga Choo-Choo. Sylvia's annoyance with the boy because of his negative personality and nondescript clothing becomes more pronounced when she hears him constantly whistling a haunting melody she cannot identify. She calls her eccentric, homosexual friend Paolo, who immediately reveals the title to be Maurice Ravel's composition "Gaspard de la Nuit."[2] Eager to please her son, Sylvia gives him a stereo set, obtains numerous records of Ravel's music and even offers to buy him a more distinctive wardrobe and a motorcycle, all of which Mauricio categorically rejects. Instead, he takes pleasure in strolling alone through the streets and parks, whistling and gazing at the people. He spends a Sunday afternoon in Vallvidrera, a suburb in the hills overlooking Barcelona, and during the days immediately following finds himself drawn back to the woods adjoining that community. The story ends with a series of strange incidents, discussed below, which explain the protagonist's enigmatic behavior and culminate with his identity crisis.

The themes underlying "Chattanooga Choo-Choo" and "Green Atom Number Five" are even more in evidence in "Gaspard de la Nuit," especially in view of the fact that Mauricio, like Humberto Peñaloza in *The Obscene Bird of Night*, is a victim of schizophrenia.[3] Thus, as his disturbed mind generates symbols, Mauricio oscillates between the search for omnipotence and nothingness, or between the desire for active participation in life and total withdrawal. These symptoms are manifested primarily through the boy's whistling which not only isolates and protects him from the encroachment of people around him, but also blots out his identity and allows him to assimilate that of others. At one point in the story he recalls how in Madrid he would go to a record shop day after day to listen to "Gaspard de la Nuit" until he had learned it perfectly. Then he would stroll through El Retiro, the city's principal park, whistling and becoming completely engrossed in the music.

The concentration that the difficulties [of the music] demanded of him pushed everything else out of his mind, and thus, although he was walking through crowded streets or through deserted parks, he remained like a blank sheet of paper, ready to receive something unknown which had to come from somewhere. (p. 254)

In spite of his efforts to efface his exterior self, he remains a "prisoner of his name, of his address, of his father, of his grandparents, and of a mother . . . who imposed on him the necessity of 'being somebody.' " Moreover, "he only succeeded in erasing all this momentarily when he whistled and, like a hunted animal, took refuge in the bottom of that lair where . . . he could wait." (p. 255)

While wandering through the streets and parks Mauricio is accustomed to following people and imagining that the tempo of his whistling somehow controls their movement. At times he

was capable of maintaining for a long while these semirelations he initiated in the streets, allowing his consciousness to absorb the other person, depriving him for a few moments of something indefinite, and yet of something which existed, but without allowing him to guess that he was being absorbed. (p. 214)

On one occasion he even whistles "Le Gibet" as he attempts to direct a gentleman's footsteps toward an imagined place of execution, and when his stratagem fails, he envisions himself holding in his hands a rope with an empty knot.

The story's principal chain of events begins when Mauricio sees in a slide viewer some pictures of Vallvidrera which cause him to experience "a refreshing sensation of light shadows and foliage, of extraordinary solitude." (p. 217) Determined to escape from his immediate reality into this realm of peace and beauty, he goes to Vallvidrera where he strolls through the woods, whistling, and hoping "to replace the fine and fresh world of the other Mauricio for the unbearable world of this Mauricio." (p. 237) While watching a football game with a group of young people, he suddenly imagines himself to be under the gaze of a pair of eyes which are attempting to release from deep within him a whistling beetle striving to take flight. He returns to his mother's apartment and looks down into the street where the sight of a boy reading a comic book renews the strange sensation he felt during the football game: "The beetle lighted up sparkling in its subterranean cave, but immobile: someone from the street was looking at him . . . and the beetle was going to climb up to the light and spread its wings." (p. 247)

Later this same evening, when Mauricio is walking home from a movie, he again senses that someone is gazing at him but this time the beetle is actually set free, obeying the eyes which direct its flight. At the same time Mauricio becomes aware of an unseen person's unsuccessful attempt to whistle "Scarbo" and feels compelled to make the necessary corrections. The next morning he returns to Vallvidrera where a similar musical exchange occurs, and soon thereafter the mysterious whistler turns out to be a beggar identical to Mauricio as well as to the youth he had seen reading a comic book. Through a series of complicated maneuvers the two young men exchange identities, the result being that Mauricio forgets how to whistle "Gaspard de la Nuit" and happily becomes a nameless nobody, whereas his indigent counterpart willingly conforms to the patterns of Sylvia's and Ramón's luxurious life style.

The denouement suggests that Mauricio's whistling represents a means of separating his true self, which emerges symbolically in the form of the beetle, from the social mask or persona he has heretofore unconsciously rejected. This interpretation is reinforced by Sylvia's complaint to her son that Ravel's music constitutes his entire essence and Mauricio's enigmatic retort that the music is not his essence but rather "a road" (p. 259) toward something he is unable to explain. And upon discovering his doppelgänger in the form of a beggar, he feels he is approaching his goal. "The important thing was that finally it was he and he would no longer have to continue inventing shadows in order to frighten away those who imposed themselves on him." (p. 263) When Mauricio actually assumes the identity of the poor, nameless youth, he reduces one side of his schizophrenic self to a nonentity that removes him from danger and frees him to create his own world of fantasy. The new Mauricio, on the other hand, by accepting the expensive clothes and motorcycle offered to him, participates in life, but his mask of conformity poses a potential threat to the self.[4]

II   *Aesthetic Elements*

The thematic unity emerging from Donoso's most recent book is paralleled by the unifying compositional elements of the three novelettes, each one of which represents an example of the well-made tale, with a variety of devices designed to sustain reader interest and literary appreciation. All three display a traditional lineal structure terminating with a climactic ending. "Chattanooga Choo-

Choo" achieves a remarkable degree of balance through its symmetrical character schematization, scenic arrangement and plot thread.
Like *This Sunday* and *The Obscene Bird of Night*, this work has four
leading figures, two men and two women, whose contrasting personalities become strangely interwined. Both the initial and final
pages describe cocktail parties attended by the same members of a
sophisticated upper-middle-class. And, whereas in the first of these
scenes the female characters' theatrical performance establishes
their alliance against Anselmo and Ramón, in the second the men's
presentation of the same number under the guiding eyes of their
mates parodies the victory of women's liberation.

All the stories introduce motifs in the opening pages that set the
tone destined to predominate and, in some cases, foreshadow the
ending. In the initial paragraph of "Chattanooga Choo-Choo" a soft,
white, nocturnal butterfly lands on Sylvia's bare shoulder, suggesting the sensuous atmosphere pervading the entire story. The description of the Ferrers' new apartment at the beginning of "Green
Atom Number Five" conveys the superficial perfection attained by the
wealthy middle-aged couple, but the empty room in their luxurious
midst alerts the reader to an ominous lacuna in their lives which,
through repetition, accumulates momentum and hastens the outcome. Similarly in "Gaspard de la Nuit" Sylvia's initial reactions to
Mauricio provide clues to the boy's personality split that occurs in
the final pages. His conventional, unimaginative clothing suggests his
unconscious desire for self-effacement whereas his whistling indicates the duality of his nature. The reader is told, for example, that
he seems to be enclosed within the perfection of the difficult piece
he whistles as if he wanted "to trace a circle around himself. . . . In
order to protect himself? To reject other people? Why?" (p. 203)
Convinced of her son's solitude, Sylvia begins to sense that the
circle drawn by his music is going "to dominate her, swallow her
up." (p. 204) ". . . it was as if Mauricio knew everything and were
capable of manipulating everything." (p. 208)

The boy's psychic world of symbols lends both aesthetic and
thematic cohesion to the work. The rope and empty knot he imagines he carries while whistling "Le Gibet" represent his urge to
dominate and destroy, the blank sheet of paper he repeatedly envisions, his longing for nothingness, and the motorcycle and yellow
shirt given to the new Mauricio by Sylvia, the materialistic values
and social conformity that pose a threat to individual identity. More

poetic are the images suggesting the emergence of Mauricio's inner self: his thick, black eyebrows compared to a swallow in flight and the beetle seeking to liberate itself.

As seen in several of his preceding works, Donoso is a master at creating mood and atmosphere, often through the injection of seemingly insignificant details. A humorous scene in "Green Atom Number Five" occurs during a moment of tension between Marta and Roberto whose material world seems to be visibly crumbling with the disappearance of their belongings. The doorbell rings and four Seventh-Day Adventists, two short, fat men and two tall, thin women, all smiling in unison, greet the Ferrers with an orchestrated "Good afternoon" and then somehow manage to worm their way into the apartment. One of the men has a mole on his bald head resembling a beetle that Roberto, in his agitation, feels certain is moving, and one of the women reveals a "false notion of sex appeal, because she wore . . . gold-plated earrings like those of a gypsy that contradicted the puritan aspect of the rest of her appearance. . . ." (p. 146) As she gazes about the elegantly furnished room, she catches sight of a naked African idol which makes her blush and lose her self-composure. Meanwhile all four have been asking questions such as, "Have you opened your heart to the word of Jesus?" (p. 148) When they begin to offer pamphlets and books to their hosts, Roberto explodes, ordering them to go away. Meekly they gather up their things but just before leaving each one picks up a valuable crystal paperweight belonging to the Ferrers who are too stunned to stop them from putting the objects into their briefcases.

The two cocktail party scenes in "Chattanooga Choo-Choo" occur in the home of Ricardo and Raimunda Roig, professional photographers who have made large sums of money from their pornographic pictures taken in Spain and sold abroad. The Roigs are the subject of much gossip because of their wealth, social prominence, and numerous love affairs but even their most severe critics never refuse their invitations. Donoso demonstrates a sharp eye and a sensitive ear for the revealing element in his sketches of the inebriated guests and their shallow, hypocritical chatter. They include a loquacious German lady named Kaethe who, attempting to imitate the latest Barcelona slang, provides a rich source of information for Anselmo (the narrator); Paolo, the ubiquitous homosexual of the group; a drunken Latin American novelist who becomes embroiled in a violent argument with his editor, smashes his fist through a windowpane and is finally thrown out; a tiny, pimply architect accompanied by his five strapping assistants "like a dictator with his bodyguards" (p. 99); a boxer-poet with a picture of Che Guevara tattooed on his chest; and a sexy blond who, after bouncing from one lap to another, vociferously announces she cannot speak a word of Spanish. It is in this milieu that Anselmo first meets Sylvia Corday, the very embodiment of the synthetic atmosphere prevailing throughout the book.

. . . her face was perfectly artificial, presenting a smooth, flat surface like an egg on which had been drawn big, dark eyes without expression or eyebrows, two patches of rouge on the cheeks, and the dark mouth near the lower extremity of the egg. (p. 18)

As Kaethe tells Anselmo, ". . . she looks as if she had been put together with plastic modules like a showcase mannequin. They say she doesn't have a face. . . . Every morning she sits down in front of the mirror and invents a face for herself. . . ." (p. 19)

III Conclusions

Sacred Families implies a condemnation of upper-middle-class society for its crass materialism, superficiality, and, most important, its disastrous effects on the individual who, like the two couples in "Chattanooga Choo-Choo," resorts to disguises for the purpose of protecting himself or imposing his will on others. Although the characters at times pride themselves on having rebelled against traditional conventions, they are, ironically, manipulated by norms they, too, have adopted without question. For example, in "Gaspard de la Nuit," Sylvia Corday scornfully alludes to the suffocating atmosphere in which her son Mauricio lives with his conservative grandparents, while she herself is upset because he does not conform to the behavioral patterns of other affluent youths. In all three works the pressures created by distorted, inflexible values lead to the self-evasion and symbolic fragmentation exemplified by Mauricio. It would seem that Donoso's horror of man's rigidly ordered reality, as seen in the lives of Roberto and Marta Ferrer in "Green Atom Number Five," is surpassed only by his horror of chaos, as shown by the frightening disintegration that follows the disappearance of Roberto's painting. Universal in its thematic content and often visual in its approach, this imaginative triptych is the most recent publication to date by a writer whose fundamental message of disillusionment and despair is softened by an acute sense of artistry and a sprinkling of sharp-edged wit, playfulness and fantasy.

CHAPTER 7

Concluding Remarks

SEVERAL obsessive themes pervade Donoso's entire literary
production, one of the most fundamental being the conflict
between reason and instinct. His descriptions of middle-class life in
particular convey the notion that the lies and false myths imposed
on man by outmoded traditions have created a Pandora's box of
suppressed emotions ready to burst forth at any moment in the form
of irrational behavior, hallucinations, or violence. A tragic conse-
quence of this situation is the grotesque distortion or complete disintegration of family relationships, a theme that appears in the early
short stories such as "Summertime" and "Fiesta en grande," as well as
in virtually all the novels. The dichotomy between reason and instinct is further illuminated by the rigidly stratified social organization which highlights the sharp differences between the sterile,
cultured rich and the downtrodden but sexually vigorous poor. The
complex relations between individuals of these two groups bring
into focus their domination of and dependence on one another, a
condition that also throws light on the lack of solidarity of the personality and its susceptibility to fragmentation. The resulting array
of masks and mutations constitutes a significant feature of the author's more recent fiction. As the characters pursue their elusive
identities, the absurdity of their efforts is underscored by the omnipresence of death, another of Donoso's major obsessions. The
confrontation with the existential void is masterfully portrayed in
"Charleston," whose protagonist fails to grasp its implications and
elects to continue along a path leading nowhere. The absurd assumes greater importance, however, in the novels where a sense of
futility and nothingness predominates.

Although the literal sketches of Donoso's short fiction impart an
overall impression of traditional realism, his characters' placid lives
are frequently disturbed by impulses over which they have little or

no control. Their irrational emotions tend to prevail in the later works, suggesting the author's deepening disenchantment with the rigidly conceived world of reason which he lampoons by uncovering the other face of reality. In the process of carrying out his attacks against false values based on absolutes, he has evolved a more subjective style and experimented extensively with avant-garde novelistic architecture, point of view and treatment of time. The result is a shift to metaphoric expression which through implication and comparison lends depth and ambiguity to objective reality. These aesthetic preoccupations tend to minimize the importance of the Chilean scene and elevate the works in question to a more abstract realm of universality. Thus, whereas *Coronation, This Sunday* and most of the short stories convey an unmistakable flavor of Chilean reality, in *Hell Has No Limits* and *The Obscene Bird of Night* the setting and culture of the author's native land, though ingeniously integrated into the fictional texture, are blurred through a prism of poeticized myth and fantasy. In a somewhat similar but more straightforward manner, the Barcelona setting of *Sacred Families* provides a backdrop for numerous scenes typifying upper-middle-class life throughout the occidental world.

Donoso is not always suitable fare for the casual reader seeking light entertainment. Though illuminated by occasional flashes of wit, irony, and fantasy, his gloomy portraits of man alone in an inhospitable universe not only convey a nostalgia for past innocence, the loss of which has contributed to the metaphysical crisis of today, but also suggest a world headed for total destruction and oblivion. The corrosion of long-established institutions is brought more sharply into focus by the protagonists who, as outsiders, impart a strong dissatisfaction with prevailing conditions and seek to liberate themselves from their oppressive environments by a wide variety of means. These include Sebastián Rengifo's withdrawal into a passive state of dreams; Andrés Abalos' flight into madness; Mathilda's rejection of rigid routine for instinctual freedom; Santelices' plunge into an imaginary forest teeming with wild beasts; Manuela's escape from a sordid milieu into a visionary realm of light, freedom and applause; Mauricio's exchange of identity for that of his whistling alter ego; and Humberto Peñaloza's psychic disintegration and death. The latter's tragic fate probably represents Donoso's most definitive statement on man and his chances for survival in the twentieth century.

The Chilean author might be described as an eclectic, having been impressed by various individuals and movements but always having shunned direct intellectual and ideological involvement. Thus, although his works illustrate the existentialist concepts of the absurd and the ever-evolving self, he rejects the more positive elements of this philosophy, recognizing little beyond despair. Likewise he joins the surrealists in their belief that Freud's irrational realm of the unconscious can be just as real as objective reality, but the surrealists' aspirations of ameliorating the human condition through their artistic endeavor would more than likely strike him as naïve. Without intending to suggest any direct influences, one can draw similarities between Donoso and some of his favorite American and European authors. Like Faulkner's, his fiction depicts vestiges of a society that has seen better days; his symbolic representations of the subconscious suggest Virginia Woolf's intuitive method; his recreation of past reality through sensory perceptions attests to his familiarity with the works of Proust; his expert manipulation of the point of view perhaps results from his avid reading of Henry James; the houses which enliven his works evoke Dickens' vividly drawn mansions; and Humberto Peñaloza's mutations and bizarre visions bring to mind Kafka's famous protagonist of *The Metamorphosis* who turns into an enormous bug.

Donoso's concern for the individual trapped in the confines of outmoded traditions and hypocritical conventions is shared by other prominent contemporary Chilean writers such as Carlos Droguett, Enrique Lafourcade, Antonio Skármeta, Alfonso Alcalde, Fernando Alegría, Jorge Edwards, Jorge Guzmán, and Guillermo Blanco. Their repudiation of existing conditions is expressed by a variety of reactions ranging from Droguett's violent rebellion to Skármeta's triumph through action and Donoso's revolt through the magical world of the inner self where reason and logic tend to disappear. In this frame of reference his monument of grotesque fantasy, *The Obscene Bird of Night,* is unique in Chilean letters and a significant event in both Latin American and world fiction.

At the present time Donoso is at the peak of his career, attracting increasing interest among critics and readers of Spanish, English, and several other languages. For this reason, it is still too soon for the literary historian to pass final judgement on his achievements. In view of the extreme pessimism pervading his fictional world, the author of the present study once asked Mr. Donoso if he considered life worth living. His answer was an unequivocal affirmative based on his belief in the glory of consciousness, imagination, and sensation. "Aside from that," he added, "there is nothing." Some readers may be depressed by Donoso's recurring insinuations of impending doom, but few will fail to appreciate his astonishing imagination, aesthetic sensitivity, and profound insight into the terrifying realities lurking beneath the surface of today's world.

Notes and References

Chapter One

1. Cedomil Goic, *La novela chilena*, 3rd ed. (Santiago, Chile, 1968), p. 163.

2. Kessel Schwartz, *A New History of Spanish American Fiction* (Coral Gables, Florida, 1972), I, 143.

3. The term *Costumbrismo* refers to a large volume of articles depicting typical scenes of Spanish life. The *Costumbristas* tended to write in a lively, humorous style, often concentrating on the picturesque aspects of their environment.

Realismo (realism), which dominated the second half of the nineteenth century, derived in part from the increasing importance of science and technology. Thus, in their novels and short stories, the realists attempted to portray contemporary conditions objectively as well as artistically.

4. Barrios is perhaps even better known for his psychological novels such as *El niño que enloqueció de amor* (The Child Who Was Maddened by Love), 1915, and *El hermano asno (Brother Ass)*, 1922.

5. María Luisa Bombal, *La última niebla* (Buenos Aires, 1969), p. 103.

6. Fernando Alegría, "La narrativa chilena (1960–70)," *Nueva Narrativa Hispanoamericana*, II, No. 1 (January 1972), 59.

7. For a detailed discussion of the Chilean generation of 1950, see Enrique Lafourcade, "La nueva literatura chilena," *Cuadernos Americanos*, CXXIII, No. 4 (July–August, 1962) 229–56.

8. *Ibid.*, p. 236.

9. Fernando Alegría, *La literatura chilena del siglo XX*, 2nd ed. (Santiago, 1962), pp. 98–99.

10. Ariel Dorfman, "Notas para un análisis marxista de la narrativa chilena en los últimos años," *Casa de las Américas*, No. 69 (Nov.–Dec. 1971) 149.

11. Goic, *op. cit.*, p. 163.

12. In June, 1973 the author of this study interviewed Donoso in his home in Calaceite, Teruel, Spain. Some of the material presented here on his

153

life and works is based on this series of interviews. For additional information on Donoso's personal life, see his "Chronology" in *Review*, No. 9 (Fall
1973), 12–19.

13. Teresa Vergara, to whom *Cuentos* is dedicated, is the model for
several of Donoso's servant characters, the most memorable being Peta
Ponce of *The Obscene Bird of Night*.

14. Donoso, "Chronology" (above, note 12), p. 12.

15. *Ibid.*, p. 13.

16. *Ibid.*, p. 13.

17. In somewhat similar circumstances Andrés Abalos, the protagonist of
Coronation, views madness as a means of escape from unbearable reality,
and his pretense of withdrawal into the world of fantasy leads to his actual
insanity.

18. "Chronology," p. 14. Misiá Elisa Grey de Abalos, the aging heroine
of *Coronation* and one of Donoso's best drawn characters, was patterned
after his grandmother.

19. *Ibid.*, p. 14.

20. Donoso's short story entitled "Dinamarquero" is based on his experiences in this desolate region.

21. "Chronology," p. 15.

22. These two stories have been republished in the November 1972 issue
of *Chasqui* (University of Wisconsin), II, No. 1, 62–72.

23. "Chronology," p. 16.

24. *Antología del nuevo cuento chileno*, Enrique Lafourcade, ed. (Santiago, Chile, 1954).

25. "Chronology," p. 19.

26. Additional information on Donoso's life may be found in the following section.

27. Although Mexico and Central America are part of North America,
critics frequently refer to Latin America as a single continent.

28. For a concise analysis of the "boom," see Emir Rodríguez Monegal,
El BOOM de la novela latinoamericana (Caracas, 1972).

29. *Ibid.*, p. 50.

30. *Ibid.*, pp. 92–93.

31. Some of these authors are Julio Cortázar of Argentina, Severo Sarduy
of Cuba (both French citizens), Carlos Fuentes of Mexico, Gabriel García
Márquez of Colombia, Mario Vargas Llosa of Peru, Augusto Roa Bastos of
Paraguay, and Guillermo Cabrera Infante of Cuba.

32. José Donoso, *Historia personal del "boom"* (Barcelona, 1972), p. 38.

33. *Ibid.*, p. 41.

34. *Ibid.*, p. 45.

35. *Ibid.*, p. 47.

36. *Ibid.*, p. 54.

37. Unlike Donoso, Fuentes is a vocal supporter of left-wing causes.

38. Donoso, *Historia personal del "boom,"* p. 45.

39. Emir Rodríguez Monegal considers the Cuban Revolution "one of the determining factors of the 'boom.'" He distinguishes between the boom in the novel and a second, ideological boom brought about principally by the Cuban cultural institution Casa de las Américas and its journal *Casa de las Américas*, which, in addition to left-wing political propaganda, has published a great deal of fine literature and literary criticism. This political and cultural revolution initiated in Cuba has been echoed by other Latin American journals such as *Marcha* in Uruguay, *Primera Plana* in Argentina, and *Siempre* in Mexico. Regarding this second boom and its effect on the original boom, Rodríguez Monegal concludes, "This is an ideological 'boom' promoted by a small country which, though under blockade, nevertheless has the international support of the socialist world, support based on the entire continent's culturally powerful left. Without this 'boom' (which has affected not only the novel but also the essay and poetry), the other one, the one everybody is talking about, perhaps never would have occurred, or would not have had the same repercussions." (*El BOOM de la novela latinoamericana*, pp. 18–22.)

40. *The Time of the Hero* is an exciting story about a group of teen-age cadets in a Lima military academy. The novel, which reaches one of its many climaxes with the murder of a cadet, suggests a parallel between, on the one hand, the corruption within the academy and its outmoded military code of discipline, and, on the other, Peruvian and Latin American societies.

41. Other Latin American novels awarded the Biblioteca Breve Prize during the 1960's are: Vicente Leñero's *Los albañiles* (The Masons); Guillermo Cabrera Infante's *Tres tristes tigres (Three Sad Tigers)*; Carlos Fuentes' *Cambio de piel (Change of Skin)*; and Adriano González León's *País portátil* (Portable Country).

42. Donoso, *Historia personal del "boom,"* pp. 89–90. *Sobre héroes y tumbas* is a highly complex existentialist novel with strong political, social, historical, and psychological overtones. The heroine and her father are descendants of a patrician family whose degeneration parallels the history of Argentina. The plot and temporal involutions convey the message that the past frequently manifests itself in the present.

43. *Ibid.*, p. 113.

44. Donoso, "Chronology," p. 18.

45. In 1970 Donoso entered his recently completed novel, *The Obscene Bird of Night*, in the competition for Seix Barral's Biblioteca Breve Prize, and it was generally believed that he would win. When the split occurred, however, and Seix Barral became Barral Editores and Seix Barral, the prize was suspended for that year.

46. Rodríguez Monegal, *op. cit.*, p. 104.

47. Donoso, *Historia personal del "boom,"* p. 124.

Chapter Two

1. Only the fourteen stories in *Cuentos* (Short Stories) are discussed in the main body of this chapter. These do not include Donoso's first two tales ("The Blue Woman" and "The Poisoned Pastries") which he published in English while studying at Princeton University (see note 22, chapter 1) or "Pasos en la noche" (Footsteps in the Night), which he wrote in 1959 while living in Buenos Aires. These three stories are treated briefly in note 23 of this chapter.

2. José Donoso, *Cuentos*, 2nd. ed. (Barcelona, 1971), p. 250. All quotations from Donoso's short stories, with the exception of "Paseo," "The Blue Woman" and "The Poisoned Pastries," are taken from *Cuentos*. Henceforth page numbers from this book will appear after each quotation.

3. In an interview conducted by Guillermo I. Castillo F., Donoso discusses his fascination with marginal beings (the very old, the very young, the neurotic, etc.) and his ideas on love, which he bases primarily on the attraction of opposites. (*Hispania*, 54, No. 4 [Dec. 1971], 958.)

4. For a brief discussion of symbiosis, see note 8, chapter 5.

5. She reacts negatively to the old man's wife and also bites her mother for no apparent reason.

6. Amada Vásquez is one of several of Donoso's characters patterned after Teresa Vergara, the servant who raised him.

7. "Paseo" was first translated to English under the same title which means "walk." The second translation bears the title "Walk."

8. Although the precise identity of the port city is unimportant, Donoso wrote "Paseo" and published it for the first time in Buenos Aires.

9. Erich Fromm discusses this Freudian theory in *The Forgotten Language* (New York, 1957), p. 56, as does Karen Horney in *The Neurotic Personality of Our Time* (New York, 1937), pp. 281–90. See also Sigmund Freud's "The Origins of Culture" in *The Modern Tradition*, edited by Richard Ellmann and Charles Feidelson, Jr. (New York, 1965), pp. 581–85.

10. José Donoso, "Paseo," *TriQuarterly*, 13/14 (Fall/Winter, 1968/1969), 309. All future quotations from "Paseo" will be followed by the page number of this issue of *TriQuarterly* where it has appeared in translation.

11. Donoso expressed this thought during an interview conducted by the author of this study. A related idea has been set forth by Erich Fromm who believes that individual isolation may be covered over by daily routine but, just as whistling in the dark does not produce light, routine does not cure fear and aloneness (*Escape From Freedom* [New York, 1969], p. 155). Fromm also states that if man becomes too enmeshed in his exterior world of routine, he can become detached from his inner self, a situation that generates feelings of isolation and despair and transforms him into an automaton, incapable of love (*The Art of Loving* [New York, 1972], pp. 72–74).

12. Carl G. Jung, "Approaching the Unconscious," *Man and His Symbols*, ed. Carl G. Jung, 9th ed. (New York, 1972), pp. 37, 72.

13. The bitch Mathilda becomes so attached to probably represents her shadow, i.e., an archetype of what Jung calls the dark side of the rational ego personality. The shadow often embodies characteristics one dislikes and usually appears as a member of the same sex. It is a vital psychic force that, if ignored, is capable of overpowering the ego.

14. Although the reader strongly suspects the fat man dies, this point is never made clear, perhaps because the insinuation of death is even more disturbing to the protagonist than its certainty.

15. The absurd element in "Charleston" is discussed in the following section dealing with irony. The existentialist concept of the absurd is discussed at the beginning of chapter 4.

16. Karen Horney's analysis of the neurotic's feelings of hostility and anxiety is applicable to Santelices:

With the capacity of hostility to generate anxiety the relation between the two is not exhausted. The process also works the other way around: anxiety in its turn, when based on a feeling of being menaced, easily provokes a reactive hostility in defense . . . . It does not matter whether anxiety or hostility has been the primary factor; the point that is highly important for the dynamics of a neurosis is that anxiety and hostility are inextricably interwoven. (*op. cit.*, pp. 74–75)

17. In "Santelices" there are some rather obvious sexual allusions that create ambiguity and generate other possible interpretations. The relationship between Doña Berta and the protagonist at times resembles that of mother and child and on other occasions acquires a vaguely sexual nature, suggesting an Oedipal relationship. The girl in the garden could also represent first a mother image and then, as Santelices' sadistic impulses become stronger, an object of sexual desire. For a more detailed analysis of this aspect of the story see George R. McMurray, " 'Santelices' de José Donoso," *El cuento hispanoamericano ante la crítica*, ed. Enrique Pupo-Walker (Madrid, 1973), pp. 215–22.

18. The surrealists believed that the apparent antagonism between the world of imagination or dreams and that of everyday reality could be reconciled by the fusion of the two realms into an absolute "surreality."

19. According to atheistic existentialism, the only branch of this philosophy referred to in this study, modern man's attempt to create a moral code he can live by in the absence of God makes his conduct the manifestation of his will to realize the missing God, even at the expense of his human qualities. Sebastián's rejection of conventions and search for his own lofty ideals lead him to abandon all meaningful contacts with his fellow men, thus denying his human side.

Hazel E. Barnes discusses the theory of man's search for the missing God in *Humanistic Existentialism* (Lincoln, Nebraska, 1959), p. 367.

20. This interpretation of "The Closed Door" evokes interesting parallels to Jorge Luis Borges' famous tale, "The Aleph" (1942), in which the narrator

experiences a moment of aesthetic revelation somewhat similar to that of Sebastián when he is able to see total reality compressed into a small disk-shaped object.

21. D. C. Muecke's *Irony* (London, 1970) provides a concise discussion of the various types of irony as well as its many possible functions in a work of art. Muecke believes that the ironic attitude derives at least in part from the erosion of religious faith and the prevailing fever of skepticism that characterizes modern man.

22. The absurd can be defined as finite man's search for reason and meaning in an infinite, unreasoning, and meaningless world. The inevitable confrontation between man and the world makes his efforts appear ridiculous and constitutes the essence of the absurd. This subject is discussed in more detail at the beginning of chapter 4.

23. The protagonist of "The Blue Woman" is a spinster whose enormous nose prevents her from achieving the happiness she craves. Even after undergoing plastic surgery she remains obsessed by her former defect and unable to adapt to her newly acquired "mask." The irony of her situation becomes strikingly apparent in the final lines when a drunk compliments her on her "pretty, smally, silly little nosey" (*Chasqui*, II, No. 1 [Nov. 1972] 66).

In "The Poisoned Pastries" the child narrator's robust, formidable father is suddenly unmasked and reduced to more human proportions by the following incident. An indigent old woman offers the child and his sister Melissa some cakes in return for the medical services performed by their father. Because the latter has refused to accept them, Melissa assumes they are poisoned, but when she questions her father about the old woman, his flushed face and obvious confusion are explained by his teasing wife, "Come now, Edward . . . Acknowledge that your stout heart was melting with sentimentality, that this simple token of gratitude embarrassed and touched you so deeply that you did not know what to do . . ." (*Chasqui*, 72).

"Footsteps in the Night" creates a nightmare of temporal involutions and doubles reminiscent of Jorge Luis Borges, the Argentine writer whom Donoso read with fascination during his extended visit in Buenos Aires. The tale's irony derives from the juxtaposition of objective reality and a nightmare, opposites which tend to fuse and nullify their respective validities. The opening paragraphs realistically describe the exhausted narrator's return to his room late at night. Soon after retiring he imagines he hears the sounds of his own footsteps approaching his boarding house a few minutes earlier. His dream world gradually intrudes more and more on reality, reflecting his loneliness through the figure of a woman he saw outlined in a window on the ground floor across the street. At the moment he witnesses his own image reach out for the woman he is awakened by her cries for help.

24. Coleman, "Some Thoughts on Donoso's Traditionalism," *Studies in Short Fiction*, VIII (Winter 1971), 155.

25. The story of a Danish immigrant and his wife Doña Concepción, a former prostitute, "The Dane's Place" describes the lonely lives of several individuals inhabiting a desolate, sparsely populated region. The narrative technique resembles that utilized in "The Güero," i.e., the central plot is told to the original first-person narrator by another first-person narrator-participant in the principal action. Thus Don Gaspard, an intimate friend of the Dane, describes the latter's first meeting with Doña Concepción, their marriage and the Dane's death several years later.

26. Expressionism originated in painting at the beginning of the twentieth century and as a literary movement flourished between 1910 and 1925, principally in Germany. (Leading expressionist writers include Franz Werfel [1890–1945], Georg Heym [1887–1912], Gottfried Benn [1886–1956], and Alfred Döblin [1878–1957].) Unlike impressionism, which emphasizes the more or less passive reception of external stimuli, expressionism utilizes violent distortions in order to express intense emotions generated from within and projected outward. Politically expressionism represents a rejection of bourgeois values.

27. The original Spanish version of "Paseo" is divided into five parts. In English the first two parts have been combined, leaving four.

28. Scene recreates a single incident by means of speech and action. It is dramatic and mimetic, showing how the action occurs. It comes closer to a living picture and presents a more intense illusion of reality. Summary can be compared to synopsis. It relates what has happened, usually after the fact.

Chapter Three

1. For further information on this point, see chapter 1: *Donoso and the "Boom."*

2. José Donoso, *Coronation* (New York, 1965), p. 228. Henceforth, all quotations from this novel will be followed immediately by the page numbers.

3. According to Freud an experience one has during the twenty-four hours prior to falling asleep often unleashes a dream referring to related incidents in one's childhood.

4. The existentialist concept of the absurd is discussed in more detail at the beginning of chapter 4.

5. For a discussion of this concept see Hazel E. Barnes, *Sartre* (Philadelphia, 1973), pp. 162–70.

6. According to existentialism each individual must accept not only his freedom to determine his essence but also full responsibility for his acts. Any form of escape from freedom or responsibility constitutes what the existentialists call "bad faith." Andrés' willful surrender to madness in order to evade reality makes him an example of bad faith.

7. The effects of Misiá Elisa's madness on Andrés recall R. D. Laing's theory that even a normal person can pick up fragments of other people's personalities and that these alien fragments can become imbedded in the individual's behavior like pieces of shrapnel in the body. The problem becomes more acute in the case of a mentally unbalanced person. (*The Divided Self* [Baltimore, 1972] , p. 105.)

8. Emir Rodríguez Monegal, "El mundo de José Donoso," *Mundo Nuevo*, No. 12 (June 1967), p. 79.

9. One should bear in mind that the following short stories were also published during this transitional period between 1957 and 1966: "The Closed Door" (1959), "Footsteps in the Night" (1959), "Paseo" (1959), "Charleston" (1960), and "Santelices" (1962). With the exception of "Footsteps in the Night" these are some of Donoso's best pieces of short fiction. Together they point to a trend away from depicting objective reality in order to explore in greater depth the subjective realms of their protagonists. For this reason they anticipate the author's conception of *This Sunday*.

10. The Chilean *empanada* is a type of pastry consisting of dough and meat.

11. Although Donoso makes use of Proust's technique of "involuntary memory" to evoke the past, his treatment of the incident is different. Proust describes, analyzes and comments on the past in a logically structured literary style, whereas Donoso immerses himself in Alvaro's inner reality, attempting to intuit the flow of his thoughts on a pre-speech level. This technique reveals a possible influence of Henri Bergson's philosophy of intuition which will be discussed at greater length in chapter 5 in connection with *The Obscene Bird of Night*.

12. José Donoso, *This Sunday* (New York, 1967), pp. 42–43. Henceforth all quotations from the novel will be followed immediately by the page numbers.

13. A Freudian technique used in psychoanalysis, free association reports whatever comes to the mind of the person being analyzed, regardless of how painful, embarrassing or irrelevant it might seem.

14. Sartre believes that human relations are based on conflict, each person tending to see himself as a free subject or center of reference and others as enslaved objects. Sooner or later he is made aware of his own self-for-others when another individual looks at him and he becomes an enslaved object in that individual's subjective center of reference. This interplay of subject-object relations often gives rise to a circle of sadism and masochism, according to Sartre.

15. Alvaro's choice of Chepa for a wife exemplifies what Freud has defined as "narcissistic identification," i.e., the selection of a love object that resembles oneself. As seen below, his subsequent withdrawal illus-

trates what Freud has called "secondary narcissism," or an incapacity for love due to the failure to emerge from the narcissistic involvement with oneself.

16. The terms "interior monologue" and "stream of consciousness" are discussed below. Also see note 27 of this chapter.

17. According to Freud, human instincts are arranged in pairs of opposites. When one feels anxiety, one attempts to sidetrack the offensive impulse by concentrating on its opposite. Chepa tries to overcome her feelings of inferiority and aloneness through relationships based on domination and, in so doing, suppresses the anxiety generated by her selfishness with a mask of altruism.

18. Four dogs also appear in *Hell Has No Limits* and *The Obscene Bird of Night* that seem to embody authority, domination, and evil. Whether they are a personal or a universal symbol is uncertain, but their presence in this scene could be based on the theory of the psyche's four-fold structure, the number four representing an archetypal symbol of wholeness or completeness. (See M. -L. von Franz, "The Process of Individuation," *Man and His Symbols*, ed. Jung, 9th ed. [New York, 1972], pp. 230–34.) If the four animals are related to this Jungian concept, Chepa's loss of her "mask" could signify the fragmentation and destruction of her personality which is anticipated during her conversation with three urchins, one of whom wants to split the "doggies" four ways. The fragmentation of the personality becomes a major theme in Donoso's subsequent works.

19. Chepa's relations with others demonstrate varying aspects of bad faith. She restricts Maya's freedom for her own selfish purposes, treats Alvaro with indifference and dominates her grandchildren and the poor people in the shantytown.

20. Marujita Bueras informs Chepa of Maya's intense dislike of Violeta. She also tells Chepa that Maya always refers to her as Misiá Chepa, "Misiá" being a term of respect used in Chile.

21. The image of the fishbowl, which appears several times in the novel, symbolizes isolation and restraint. On one occasion the grandson imagines his grandfather is swimming alone in a bowl while others make fun of him from the outside (p. 12).

22. *Roncafort* has an amusing connotation in Spanish. *Roncar* means to "snore" and *fort* is close to *fuerte* meaning "strong" or "loud". In Chile the idiom *Ese ronca fuerte* (That fellow snores loudly) is the rough equivalent to *He's a "big shot."*

23. The medallions appear again with similar symbolic connotations in *The Obscene Bird of Night*.

24. The existentialists' "serious world," which seems to be mocked here, is the society into which one is born with a particular place prepared for him and in which absolute values are pre-established and not to be questioned.

25. The fact that the events occur on the Sabbath, the rituals of which signify salvation, freedom, and harmony, emerges as ironic in view of the existential anguish and psychological and social tensions depicted. This also applies to *Hell Has No Limits*.

26. For a brief discussion of the differences between summary and scene see note 28, chapter 2.

27. There is some confusion about the exact meaning of the terms "stream of consciousness" and "interior monologue." As a technique the two terms often are given identical meanings, "interior monologue" being used more frequently in continental Europe than in English-speaking countries. If the stream of consciousness appears in first person, it is sometimes referred to as a direct interior monologue (emanating directly from the character's psyche), but if the author captures the character's internal thoughts in the third person, the technique is sometimes called the indirect interior monologue. The direct and indirect interior monologues, then, are two facets of the more general terms "interior monologue" or "stream of consciousness" which are used interchangeably in this study.

28. The grotesque usually involves exaggerated distortion, monstrous physical abnormalities, and the clash between incompatibles such as mirth and horror. Grotesque art is more prevalent in societies marked by strife, radical change or disorientation. (For a concise discussion of this subject see Philip Thompson, *The Grotesque*, [London, 1972.])

Hell Has No Limits also ends with a grotesque image which, like that of *This Sunday*, suggests a disintegrating world.

29. Just prior to Chepa's entrance to the shantytown in search of Maya she catches sight of several *animitas*.

Chapter Four

1. The theme of the Fall is reinforced by the quotation from Christopher Marlowe's *Doctor Faustus* which prefaces the novel. To Dr. Faustus' question, "Tell me, where is the place that men call hell?" Mephostophilis replies,

> Under the heavens.
> . . .
> Within the bowels of these elements
> Where we are tortured, and remain for ever.
> Hell hath no limits, nor is circumscribed
> In one self place; but where we are is hell,
> And where hell is, there must we ever be. . . . (p. 149)

2. Don Alejo also bears certain resemblances to three gods of classical mythology: Saturnus, the deity who introduces the cultivation of the vine and whose reign became known as the Golden Age; Hades, the heartless god of the underworld; and Dionysus, the god of wine and ecstasy.

According to Roman mythology, a festival known as the Saturnalia was held annually in honor of Saturnus and a sacrifice was made. This brings to mind the celebration of Don Alejo's election to the Senate and the "sacrifice" of Manuela, who is thrown into the canal.

In her unpublished Master's thesis entitled *Hell Hath No Limits* (Colorado State University, 1970), Hallie Taylor has pointed out some striking similarities between the House of Hades and the setting of *Hell Has No Limits*. She also points out that Dionysus bestows the gift of wine on those who welcome him as well as the gift of ecstasy whereby one may be freed from the fetters of one's own personality. Big Japonesa welcomes Don Alejo into her house and she alone in the village receives wine from him without charge. The gift of ecstasy enables Manuela to transcend the bounds of the novel's sordid physical environment.

3. José Donoso, *Hell Has No Limits* in *Triple Cross* (New York, 1972), p. 154. All subsequent quotations from this novel will be followed immediately by the page numbers.

4. Don Alejo's domination of the citizens of Estación El Olivo also reflects the subject-object relationship Sartre considers fundamental in human associations. For a brief discussion of this relationship, see note 14, chapter 3.

5. Although he is a man, Manuela is usually referred to as "she" in the novel. In this study the feminine pronoun will also be used except on rare occasions to avoid ambiguity as, for example, when "he" alludes to Manuela in his role as Japonesita's father.

6. It should be pointed out that although Don Alejo is depicted from many exterior points of view, he emerges as a flat character because, unlike Pancho, Manuela, and Japonesita, he is never seen from within. This cubistic method of portraying him from different angles is effective because it reinforces his inscrutable, contradictory nature.

7. Jung, *op. cit.*, p. 62.

8. Sartre calls conscious reality Being-for-itself and nonconscious reality Being-in-itself. Being-for-itself is free to make choices and subject to dynamic change whereas Being-in-itself is represented by the static permanence of things in nature. According to the French philosopher, man desires both the surety of things in nature and the free choice of consciousness, or he wants to escape the responsibility of Being-for-itself and still remain superior to Being-in-itself. Sartre concludes that man attempts to achieve absolute Being by vainly pursuing the impossible "in-itself-for-itself" or the missing God. For a more detailed discussion of this theory, see Hazel E. Barnes, *Humanistic Existentialism* (Lincoln, Nebraska, 1959), pp. 30–33, 112–21.

9. In view of Pancho's subsequent behavior with Don Alejo, this incident constitutes an empty threat, but it nevertheless foreshadows the truck driver's sadistic treatment of Manuela, a weaker individual.

10. Just as Carlos Gros represents a foil for Andrés Abalos in *Coronation*, the strong, independent Octavio contrasts sharply with Pancho.

11. Pancho's situation recalls that of Andrés Abalos who rejects religion and dreams repeatedly of falling off a truncated bridge into the abyss of nothingness. Andres' attraction to and rejection of his grandmother's mansion is also similar to Pancho's ambivalent attitude toward Estación El Olivo.

12. Manuela's struggle to escape the confines of her environment also recalls the surrealists' revolt against bourgeois society and their efforts to illuminate the dark side of existence through beauty, imagination and total liberty. The Chilean scholar Hernán Vidal's book, *José Donoso: surrealismo y rebelión de los instintos* (Barcelona, 1972), deals at length with surrealism in Donoso's novels. The present study treats this subject in the following chapter, which is dedicated to *The Obscene Bird of Night*.

13. In this entire passage, because of Manuela's extreme fright, she refers to herself with both masculine and feminine pronouns.

14. This monster also evokes Cerberus, the three-headed dog in Greek mythology that watched over the entrance to the infernal regions of the dead.

15. A characteristic often associated with Latin American males, *machismo* manifests itself in an overt display of valor and masculinity.

16. Don Alejo is seen through Manuela's, Pancho's, Japonesita's, and Big Japonesa's minds; Pancho is viewed by Manuela and Japonesita; Japonesita is reflected by Manuela, Pancho, and Miss Lila (the post-office clerk); and Big Japonesa is recalled by Japonesita and Manuela. This technique resembles what Norman Friedman has called "multiple selective omniscience," i.e., the method of allowing the story to come directly through the minds of the characters. The result is a tendency toward scene rather than narrative summary, which is the case in *Hell Has No Limits*. (See Norman Friedman, "The Point of View in Fiction: The Development of a Critical Concept," *The Novel: Modern Essays in Criticism*, ed. Robert Murray Davis [Englewood Cliffs, N.J., 1969], p. 160).

17. It will be recalled that in *Coronation* Misiá Elisa's pink shawl became for Andrés a sexual symbol linked mysteriously with the pink palms of Estela's hands. A unifying element of design, Japonesita's shawl appears in both the opening and closing lines of the novel.

18. *Chiaroscuro* is the Italian technical term for light and shade. This technique, which was particularly popular during the sixteenth and seventeenth centuries, usually illuminates the portrait's central figure and obscures the remaining portions in deep shadows. These violent contrasts heighten emotional tension and create an air of depression and imminent death. (Caravaggio, Rembrandt, and Georges de la Tour are three of the painters Donoso admires most.)

19. This word portrait was quite possibly inspired by Georges de la Tour (1593–1652), a French painter of many candlelight scenes.

20. Donoso admitted to the author of this study that Don Céspedes does represent Charon. The initial clue to this piece of information is the name of the canal (Palos) which means "sticks" in English—thus the River Styx. A somewhat mysterious figure, Don Céspedes makes the difficult crossing of the canal and easily finds his way through the thickets between Don Alejo's estate and Estación El Olivo.

Chapter Five

1. Approximately fifty pages of the Spanish edition have been eliminated from the English translation. This has made the novel more concise and increased its impact.

2. According to critic Fernando Alegría, the antinovel in Chilean literature has its roots in several relatively unknown works including *Sátiro* (1939), by Vicente Huidobro, and *Un año* (1934), *Ayer* (1935), and *Miltín* (1935), by Juan Emar, all of which break with conventional realism and display avant-garde techniques. (*Literatura y revolución* [Mexico City, 1971], pp. 18, 197.)

3. José Donoso, *The Obscene Bird of Night* (New York, 1973), p. 31. Henceforth page numbers of passages quoted from the novel will appear immediately after each quotation.

4. French poet André Breton (1896–1966) is recognized as the leading figure of the surrealist movement. In addition to Freud's theories, the surrealists accepted Jung's concept of the collective unconscious.

5. Jung divides the Freudian unconscious into two basic levels, the personal or upper level, and the collective or lower level. According to Jung schizophrenia yields an immense harvest of collective symbols which can also appear in dreams occurring deep in the individual's unconscious. (See Carl B. Jung, *The Psychogenesis of Mental Disease* [New York, 1960], pp. 241–43.)

6. The persona is what Jung calls the outer layer of the personality which the individual displays in society. It is identified with the conscious ego.

7. For a concise discussion of this mental illness, see Joseph Campbell, "Schizophrenia—the Inward Journey," *Myths to Live By* (New York, 1972), pp. 207–39. Campbell states that the patient, prior to his total withdrawal from reality as described above, may see himself in two roles, first as an outsider (Humberto on La Rinconada comes to mind) and then as a savior, which is one of Mudito's roles in the Casa.

8. This passage also anticipates the symbiotic union between Humberto and Don Jerónimo which is destined to occur in Humberto's imagination.

Symbiosis results from a person's inability to bear the burden of the individual self, causing him to cast off the burden through dependency on another person. The symbiotic union can also become a sadomasochistic relationship, as it does in the case of Jerónimo and Humberto.

9. According to Jung, the shadow can become a positive factor in the personality if it is properly integrated into one's life. It can become dangerous, as in the case of Jerónimo and Boy, if it is ignored or misunderstood. For a discussion of the shadow, see Carl G. Jung, *The Portable Jung* (New York, 1971), pp. 144–48.

10. In 1799 Spanish painter Francisco de Goya y Lucientes published a series of eighty etchings entitled *Los caprichos* (Caprices) in which he utilized the popular imagery of caricature in order to attack political, social and religious abuses. The caption for number 43 of these etchings is "The sleep of reason produces monsters." (*Los caprichos*, Dover ed. [New York, 1969].)

11. Humberto's operation and hallucinations are based on an episode from the author's life. See chapter 1, *Biography*.

12. Based on a myth of the Araucanian Indians of Chile, the *imbunche* refers to a child that has been stolen by witches and transformed into a monster with all its orifices sewed shut.

13. Donoso told the author of this study that in creating Doña Inés he had in mind certain characteristics of Diana, the Roman moon goddess and mother deity who helped women in childbirth. In this scene the moon plays a mysterious role in Boy's conception.

14. Donoso expressed this idea in an interview with the author of this study. Like Jung, he sees life as a kind of masquerade, the individual wearing a mask for each role he is obliged to play in his daily existence.

15. Donoso has expressed his taste for symmetry in his works. In an interview with Emir Rodríguez Monegal he stated, " . . . in my novels I always tend toward symmetry. . . . I have a real passion for the artificial." ("José Donoso: La novela como 'happening,' " *Revista Iberoamericana*, XXXVII, Nos. 76–77 [July–December 1971], 526.)

16. In an interview with the author of this study Donoso declared, "I consider the role of symbols in my work the most important element, especially in *The Obscene Bird of Night* which is a notation of symbols. Working with symbols rather than with natural phenomena gives the novel greater ambiguity." (June 1973)

17. Jerónimo's world of rigid categories is similar to the existentialists' "serious world" which is defined in note 24, chapter 3.

18. Both surrealism and existentialism represent reactions against the excesses of rationalism and science which are blamed for the horrors of twentieth-century wars. Both movements stress the individual's freedom to determine his own destiny and reject all traditions, including Christian dogma, that prevent one from realizing one's capabilities. Both groups are

identified with the political left, Breton having belonged to the Communist Party during the 1930's and Sartre having supported it off and on for years. Surrealists and existentialists recognize the instability of the human consciousness which they consider to be in a constant state of flux. Of the two movements, existentialism has evolved a more systematic philosophy, due primarily to the influence of Sartre.

19. The concept of the absurd is discussed at the beginning of chapter 4.

20. Because of their distortions of reality, these episodes also represent surrealistic visions of the protagonist's unconscious. Their philosophical implications, however, are of a more existential nature.

21. Another difference between Don Alejo and Don Jerónimo is that the former emerges as a flat character who is never seen from within whereas the latter's interior monologues make him more complex. Both characters are equally effective, Don Alejo remaining inscrutable and Don Jerónimo gradually assuming human proportions.

22. For a brief discussion of the Sartrean subject-object relationship, see note 14, chapter 3.

23. For a more complete discussion of Sartre's theory of Being-in-itself and Being-for-itself, see note 8, chapter 4.

24. Primarily a poetic movement, Modernism lasted from the 1880's until approximately 1916 when its leader, Nicaraguan poet Rubén Darío died. Initially the movement was characterized by the rejection of bourgeois values, the perfection of literary form, and the use of symbolic imagery, musical sounding phrases, and innovative metrical rhythms. Subsequently, the Modernist poets also stressed philosophical, political, and social themes.

25. This information was given by Donoso to the author of this study. Teiresias was struck with blindness by the gods for seeing what he was not supposed to see, but subsequently was granted the gift of prophecy and the ability to understand the voices of the birds. Like Mudito, he was both male and female. Mudito never loses his sight but he constantly fears Jerónimo will deprive him of it.

26. The walls of Mudito's room have been covered with newspapers which Damiana reads aloud (pp. 102–3). This collage technique, in a sense, brings the world into the protagonist's lodgings.

27. The year of Jerónimo's return is probably 1916 since concern is expressed over the outcome of the Battle of Verdun (p. 137).

28. The temporal realm nevertheless becomes blurred, as it so often does in dreams, when one calculates that Boy's birth must have occurred in 1922 and Jerónimo's death fifteen years later. Yet it is implied throughout the novel that Jerónimo lives into the 1960's.

29. The four leading characters live on La Rinconada for approximately six years prior to Boy's birth, after which they presumably move to the city. Although the Chilean capital is never mentioned, Donoso told the author of

this study that the Casa was inspired by an old convent he once visited in Santiago and that La Rinconada was patterned after an estate he frequented as a child.

30. This image acquires a touch of irony when it is recalled that before retiring to the Casa, María Benítez was Don Clemente's cook and, because she prepared weekly luncheons for influential politicians, was occasionally caricatured in the newspapers as the "embodiment of the oligarchy, a lady using a huge spoon to stir a cauldron labeled with the country's name." (p. 136)

31. Mudito need have no fear that Don Jerónimo will enter the Casa. He never comes near the institution, perhaps because of his fear of the dark side of life which it reflects.

32. It will be recalled that Mudito has just covered over the openings in the Casa to keep Jerónimo out.

33. Although Narcissus fell in love with his own reflection, Don Jerónimo's tragic fate evokes Narcissus' suicidal death by drowning which, according to Erich Neumann, symbolizes the dissolution of the ego consciousness. (The Origin and History of Consciousness [Princeton, 1971], p. 96.) Inasmuch as the ego consciousness is identified with the persona, the death of Don Jerónimo (Humberto's persona) signifies the collapse of Humberto's ego and clears the way for his total psychic disintegration.

34. Don Jerónimo dies two different deaths in the novel, one by drowning which constitutes the demise of the character whose human weakness makes him more real than fictional. The other death is related twice, in identical passages (pp. 129–30, 407), and represents a part of the historical biography Humberto is writing. This episode concerns the traditional death of a flawless, fictitious statesman revered by his countrymen. The fact that it is repeated twice indicates Humberto's preoccupation with his book.

35. Although she was an illiterate servant, Brígida had an uncanny ability to play the stockmarket and became very rich. She worked for Misiá Raquel Ruiz who ran herself ragged looking after Brígida's investments and, after her servant's death, arranged to have a home built to replace the Casa.

36. It should be pointed out that Mudito's experience in this burlap limbo resembles the kind of existence anticipated for Boy after his brain surgery, thus once again suggesting the fusion of these two identities.

37. In his Second Manifesto of Surrealism (1930), André Breton defines in the following manner the point the surrealists hoped to determine: "Everything leads us to believe there exists a certain point in the mind in which life and death, real and imaginary, past and future, communicable and incommunicable, high and low cease to be perceived as contradictions." (See J. H. Matthews, An Introduction to Surrealism [University Park, Pennsylvania, 1965], p. 48.)

38. According to C. G. Jung, the Christ child is an archetypal image that

indicates man's desire to restore his innocence lost by the Fall. (See Jung, *Psyche and Symbol* [New York, 1958], p. 36.)

39. The title is taken from a letter written by Henry James Sr. to his sons Henry and William.

Every man who has reached even his intellectual teens begins to suspect that life is no farce . . . that it flowers and fructifies on the contrary out of the profoundest tragic depths of the essential dearth in which its subject's roots are plunged. The natural inheritance of everyone who is capable of spiritual life is an unsubdued forest where the wolf howls and the obscene bird of night chatters. (Preface to *The Obscene Bird of Night*)

40. This chapter is also interesting because of its ingenious technique. Mother Benita's unhappy life, the ironically reversed relationship between Misiá Raquel Ruiz and her servant Brígida, and Father Azócar's theft of the lamp are interwoven in a long interior monologue which, though filtered through Mother Benita's psyche, is conveyed to the reader by Mudito. The result is the revelation of several consciousnesses operating simultaneously on different levels.

41. These passages were the first parts of the novel to be written and, according to Donoso, approximate the noble, classical style of Isak Dinesen, some of whose works he translated in the early 1960's.

42. One of Di Chirico's most famous paintings expressing the labyrinthian nature of the unconscious is *Anxious Journey* (1913), which pictures a series of gloomy, sharply outlined passages set in a fathomless vacuum. Di Chirico (1888) was an influential precursor of surrealism and usually figures prominently in most discussions of the movement.

43. At the end of the novel, when Mudito is trying to bite his way out of the sacks, the old woman who throws him onto the bonfire mends each hole he makes "as if she were embroidering initials on the finest batiste instead of sewing burlap." (p. 436) This recalls the handkerchiefs Peta Ponce gives to Don Jerónimo which are "of the finest batiste, with handstitched borders and initials so exquisitely embroidered." (p. 148)

Chapter Six

1. José Donoso, *Tres novelitas burguesas* (Barcelona, 1973), p. 86. Henceforth all quotations from this book will be followed immediately by the page numbers.

2. One of France's most significant modern composers, Maurice Ravel (1875–1937) is known for his virtuosity and refinement. Among his best piano compositions is "Gaspard de la Nuit" (1908) which consists of three movements: "Ondine," "Le Gibet," and "Scarbo." This composition is a musical illustration of a work of the same title by the nineteenth-century

French romantic poet Aloysius Bertrand. Although "Ondine" and "Scarbo" are mentioned in Donoso's novelette, "Le Gibet" (The Gallows) plays the most important role. The literary text of "Le Gibet" sets forth macabre images of an executed man hanging from a gallows.

3. The symptoms of schizophrenia are described in the preceding chapter.

4. The new Mauricio adopts his counterpart's habit of whistling, an indication that he may repeat the former Mauricio's behavioral pattern. In the final scene, moreover, when the two youths meet for the last time, the beggar sees fear in the new Mauricio's eyes.

Selected Bibliography

1. Novels (in chronological order)
Coronación. Santiago: Nascimento, 1957.
Este domingo. Santiago: Editorial Zig-Zag, 1966.
El lugar sin límites. Mexico: Joaquín Mortiz, 1966.
El obsceno pájaro de la noche. Barcelona: Editorial Seix Barral, 1970.

2. Short stories (in chronological order)
"The Blue Woman," *MSS* (Princeton University literary review), III, No. 1 (November 1950), 3–7.
"The Poisoned Pastries," *MSS*, III, No. 3 (May 1951), 3–8.
"China," *Antología del nuevo cuento chileno*, ed. Enrique Lafourcade. Santiago: Editorial Zig-Zag, 1954.
Veraneo y otros cuentos. Santiago: Editorial Universitaria, 1955. Contains: "Veraneo," "Tocayos," "El güero," "Una señora," "Fiesta en grande," "Dos cartas," "Dinamarquero."
Dos cuentos. Santiago: Editorial Guardia Vieja, 1956. Contains: "El hombrecito," "Ana María."
"La puerta cerrada," *Cuentos de la generación del 50*, ed. Enrique Lafourcade. Santiago: Editorial del Nuevo Extremo, 1959.
"Pasos en la noche," *Américas*, XI, No. 2 (February 1959), 21–23.
"Paseo," *Sur*, No. 261 (November–December 1959), 17–33.
El charleston. Santiago: Editorial Nascimento, 1960. Contains: "El charleston," "La puerta cerrada," "Ana María," "Paseo," "El hombrecito."
"Santelices," *Revista Universidad de México*, XVI (July 1962), 13–19.
Los mejores cuentos de José Donoso. Santiago: Editorial Zig-Zag, 1965. Contains: "Veraneo," "Tocayos," "El güero," "Una señora," "Fiesta en grande," "Dos cartas," "Dinamarquero," "El charleston," "La puerta cerrada," "Ana María," "Paseo," "El hombrecito," "China," "Santelices."
Cuentos. Barcelona: Seix Barral, 1971. Contains the fourteen stories included in *Los mejores cuentos de José Donoso.*

171

3. Novelettes

Tres novelitas burguesas. Barcelona: Editorial Seix Barral, 1973. Contains:
"Chatanooga Choochoo," "Átomo verde número cinco," "Gaspard de
la nuit."

4. Autobiography

Historia personal del "boom." Barcelona: Editorial Anagrama, 1972.
"Chronology," *Review,* No. 9 (Fall 1973), 12–20.

5. Translations to English

"Footsteps in the Night," *Américas,* XI, No. 2 (Feb. 1959), 21–23.
"The 'Hombrecito,'" trans. Robert Roland, *Granta,* LXIX, No. 1237 (June
1964), 10–13.
Coronation. Trans. Jocasta Goodwin. New York: Knopf, 1965.
This Sunday. Trans. Lorraine O'Grady Freeman. New York: Knopf, 1967.
"Ana María," trans. J. M. Cohen, *Latin American Writing Today,* ed. J. M.
Cohen. Baltimore: Penguin Books, 1967.
"Paseo," trans. Lorraine O'Grady Freeman, *The TriQuarterly Anthology of
Contemporary Latin American Literature,* eds. José Donoso and Wil-
liam Henkin, 13–14 (Fall–Winter, 1968–69), 307–24.
Hell Has No Limits. Trans. Suzanne Jill Levine and Hallie Taylor. In *Triple
Cross.* New York: Dutton, 1972.
The Obscene Bird of Night. Trans. Hardie St. Martin and Leonard Mades.
New York: Knopf, 1973.
The Boom in Spanish American Literature A Personal History. Trans. Greg-
ory Kolovakos. New York: Columbia University Press in association
with the Center for Inter-American Relations, 1977.
Charleston & Other Stories. Trans. Andrée Conrad. Boston: David R.
Godine, Publisher, 1977. Contains: "Ana María," "Summertime,"
"The Güero," "A Lady," "The Walk," "The Closed Door," "The
Dane's Place," "Charleston," "Santelices."
Sacred Families. Trans. Andrée Conrad. New York: Knopf, 1977.

SECONDARY SOURCES

ALEGRÍA, FERNANDO. "La narrativa chilena (1960–1970)," *Nueva Narrativa
Hispanoamericana,* II, No. 1 (January 1972), 59–63. Comments on
recent Chilean fiction and its reflection of the moral crisis of the
1960's.
BORINSKY, ALICIA. "Repeticiones y máscaras: *El obsceno pájaro de la
noche,*" *Modern Language Notes,* 88, No. 2 (March 1973), 281–93.
Emphasizes elusive reality in Donoso's novels.
COLEMAN, ALEXANDER. "Some Thoughts on Donoso's Traditionalism,"
Studies in Short Fiction, VIII (Winter 1971), 155–58. Brief comments

Selected Bibliography   173

on thematic and aesthetic aspects of Donoso's stories and first three novels.

DÉLANO, POLI. "Apuntes sobre lo que se va dejando de llamar 'las neuvas hornadas' de la narrativa chilena," *Casa de las Américas*, No. 75 (November–December 1972), 147–51. Comparisons drawn between the Chilean literary generations of 1938, 1950, and the 1960's with special emphasis on political and social attitudes.

DORFMAN, ARIEL. "Temas y problemas de la narrativa chilena actual," *Chile, hoy*, by several authors. Mexico City: Siglo XXI Editores, 1970, pp. 385–407. A discussion of reactions to the harsh realities of today as seen in Chilean fiction of the 1960's. Also contains a short bibliography of outstanding works of the decade.

GOIC, CEDOMIL. *La novela chilena*. Santiago: Editorial Universitaria, 1968, pp. 163–76. A study of the literary techniques and characters of *Coronation*.

GOLDEMBERG, ISAAC. "*Coronación* de José Donoso o los límites del aislamiento," *Mundo Nuevo*, No. 36 (June 1969), 74–80. An analysis of the physical, emotional and spiritual isolation in Donoso's first novel.

HUNEEUS, CRISTIÁN. "El mundo de José Donoso," *Amaru*, No. 4 (October–December 1967), 72–77. A discussion of the major themes and techniques in the stories, *Coronation* and *This Sunday*.

LAFOURCADE, ENRIQUE. "La nueva literatura chilena," *Cuadernos Americanos*, CXXIII, No. 4 (1962), 229–56. A panorama of twentieth-century Chilean literature with detailed comments and bibliographical information on the generation of 1950.

MOIX, ANA MARÍA. "Prólogo," *Cuentos*, by José Donoso. Barcelona: Seix Barral, 1971, pp. 9–21. An analysis of the themes and techniques in Donoso's works, from the traditional realism of the stories to the avant-garde surrealism of *The Obscene Bird of Night*.

MULLER, ANITA L. "La dialéctica de la realidad en *El obsceno pájaro de la noche*," *Nueva Narrativa Hispanoamericana*, II, No. 2 (September 1972), 93–100. A study of psychological and symbolic elements in Donoso's novel.

PROMIS OJEDA, JOSÉ. "La desintegración del orden en la novela de José Donoso," *La novela hispanoamericana, descubrimiento e invención de América*. ed. Ricardo Vergara. Valparaíso: Ediciones Universitarias, 1973, pp. 209–38. A detailed examination of social and psychological disintegration in Donoso's novels.

RODRÍGUEZ MONEGAL, EMIR. "El mundo de José Donoso," *Mundo Nuevo*, No. 12 (June 1967), 77–85. An analysis of Donoso's stories and first three novels with particular stress on the irrational impulses lurking beneath the calm surface of bourgeois life.

———. "La novela como 'happening,'" *Revista Iberoamericana*, Nos. 76–77

(July–December 1971), 517–36. An interview in which Donoso's comments lend insight into the meaning of *The Obscene Bird of Night*.

SARDUY, SEVERO. "Writing/Transvestism," *Review*, No. 9 (Fall, 1973), 31–33. Views *Hell Has No Limits* as a grotesque world of masks and sexual inversion.

STABB, MARTIN S. "The Erotic Mask: Notes on Donoso and the New Novel," *Symposium*, XXX, No. 3 (Summer 1976), 170–79. Sexuality in *The Obscene Bird of Night* is seen as a dark force, tinged with the satanic, lurking behind the mask.

TATUM, CHARLES M. "The Child Point of View in Donoso's Fiction," *Journal of Spanish Studies: Twentieth Century*, I, No. 3 (Winter 1973), 187–96. Stresses the loss-of-innocence theme and the perversion of values as the child becomes part of the adult world.

————. "*El obsceno pájaro de la noche:* The Demise of a Feudal Society," *Latin American Literary Review*, I, No. 2 (Spring 1973), 99–105. Highlights social disintegration, symbolism and ambiguity in Donoso's most ambitious work.

VIDAL, HERNÁN. *José Donoso: Surrealismo y rebelión de los instintos.* Barcelona: Ediciones Aubí, 1972. A detailed study of the novels based on Jungian theories and Donoso's exploration of the human psyche.

WEBER, FRANCES WYERS. "La dinámica de la alegoría: *El obsceno pájaro de la noche,* de José Donoso," *Hispamérica*, IV, Nos. 11–12 (1975), 23–31. A discussion of the allegorical themes, with special emphasis on the struggle for power, in *The Obscene Bird of Night*.

BIBLIOGRAPHICAL SOURCES

HASSETT, JOHN J., Charles M. Tatum and Kirsten Nigro. "Bibliography-José Donoso," *Chasqui*, II, No. 1 (November 1972), 15–30. A summary of Donoso's life and a bibliography of primary and secondary sources.

McMURRAY, GEORGE R. "José Donoso, Bibliography-Addendum," *Chasqui*, III, No. 2 (February 1974), 23–44. Additional bibliographical material including many newspaper reviews.

Index

Absurd, the, 43, 50, 90–107, 120, 136, 148, 150, 158n22; *see also* Existentialism, Sartre, Sartre's psychology
Aguirre, Margarita, 20; *El huésped*, 19
Agustín, José, 33
Alegría, Ciro: *Broad and Alien Is the World*, 16
Alegría, Fernando, 17, 18, 19, 150; *Literatura y revolución*, 165n2
Andrés (*Coronation*), 59, 60, 61, 62, 63, 64, 65, 66, 67, 68, 69, 70, 71, 87, 149
Angurrientismo, 15, 16
Araucanian myth, 166n11; *see also imbunche*
Arenas, Reynaldo, 33
Arguedas, José María: *Los ríos profundos*, 26
Art Nouveau, 67–68
Asturias, Miguel Angel: *El señor Presidente*, 26
Azuela, Mariano: *The Underdogs*, 16

Barnes, Hazel E.: *Humanistic Existentialism*, 157n19, 163n8; *Sartre*, 159n5
Barrios, Eduardo: *Gran señor y rajadiablos*, 16; *El hermano asno*, *El niño que enloqueció de amor*, 153n4
Beckett, Samuel, 91, 108
Bergson, Henri, 17, 72, 121–22, 124, 160n11
Bertrand, Aloysius, 169–70n2
Big Japonesa (*Hell Has No Limits*), 89, 93–94, 98, 101, 162–63n2
Bioy Casares, Adolfo, 26, 28
Blanco, Guillermo, 20, 150
Bombal, María Luisa: *House of Mist*, 17–18
"Boom," the, 25–33, 155n39

Borges, Jorge Luis, 26, 28, 91, 157n20
Boy (*The Obscene Bird of Night*), 108, 109, 112, 115, 118, 119, 120, 125, 126, 130, 131, 136, 137, 166n13, 168n36
Breton, André, 165n4, 166–67n18; *Second Manifesto of Surrealism*, 168n37
Brunet, Marta, 16
Bryce Echeñique, Alfredo, 33
Bullrich, Silvina, 28

Campbell, Joseph: *Myths to Live By*, 165n7
Camus, Albert, 20, 90–91, 92
Caravaggio, Michelangelo Merisi da, 106, 164n18
Carpentier, Alejo, 30; *The Kingdom of This World*, 26; *The Lost Steps*, 28
Casa de las Américas, 155n39
Cerberus, 164n14
Charon, 107, 165n20
Chepa (*This Sunday*), 72, 74, 75, 76, 77, 78, 79, 80, 81, 82, 83, 84, 85, 86, 87, 88, 160n15, 161n18, 161n19
Chiaroscuro, 164n18
Chilean *Criollistas*, 16
Chirico, Giorgio di, 135; "Anxious Journey," 169n42
Coleman, Alexander, 53
Cortázar, Julio, 25, 91, 108
Costumbrismo, 15, 153n3
Criollismo, 15, 16, 18

Darío, Rubén, 27, 167n24
D'Halmar, Augusto, 17
Diana (the goddess), 166n13
Dickens, Charles, 150
Dinesen, Isak, 169n41
Dionysus, 162–63n2

Doña Inés (*The Obscene Bird of Night*),
    108, 109, 110, 113, 114, 115, 116, 117,
    118, 119, 123, 126, 128, 129, 130, 133,
    136, 137, 166n13
Don Alejo (*Hell Has No Limits*), 89, 90,
    92–93, 94, 95, 96, 97, 98, 100, 101,
    102, 104, 105, 106, 107, 120, 162–
    63n2, 163n4, 163n6, 167n21
Don Alvaro (*This Sunday*), 72–73, 74,
    75, 76, 79, 81, 82, 83, 84, 85, 86, 87,
    106n11, 160n15
Don Jerónimo (*The Obscene Bird of
    Night*), 108, 109, 111, 112, 115, 116,
    117, 118, 119, 120, 121, 122, 123, 124,
    125, 126, 127, 128, 129, 130, 131, 135,
    136, 137, 165–66n8, 167n21, 168n33,
    169n43
Donoso, José, and religion, 22; and the
    "Boom," 25–33; as member of the
    generation of 1950, 18–20; at Congress
    of Intellectuals in Concepción, 30; at
    Princeton, 22–23; at the Grange, 21,
    29–30; biography, 20–25; birth, child-
    hood and youth, 20–22; career as
    journalist, 24; career as teacher,
    23–24; early career as writer, 23–25;
    early readings, 22; Guggenheim
    Awards, 24, 25; illness, 21; in Col-
    orado, 24; in Iowa, 24; in Magallanes,
    22; in Mexico, 32; in Spain, 24, 25

WORKS:
"Ana María," 35–36, 54, 56
"Blue Woman, The," 23, 156n1,
    158n23
*Boom in Spanish American Literature
    A Personal History, The*, 25, 26, 32
Casa de campo, 25
"Charleston," 41–43, 49, 50, 54, 56,
    148
"Chattanooga Choo-Choo," 138–39,
    141, 143, 144, 145, 146
"Closed Door, The," 46–48, 50–51,
    54, 56, 157n20
"China," 23, 34, 35, 53, 56
Coronation, 19, 23, 27, 28, 32, 59–71,
    72, 87, 88, 149
"Dane's Place, The," 54, 56, 159n25
"Dos cartas," 36, 54

"Footsteps in the Night," 28, 156n1,
    158n23
"Fiesta en grande," 45–46, 49, 54, 148
"Gaspard de la Nuit," 141–43, 144,
    146
"Green Atom Number Five," 139–40,
    141, 144, 145, 146
"Güero, The," 37–38, 54, 56, 159n25
Hell Has No Limits, 32, 89–107, 120,
    149, 161n18, 162n28, 162–63n2,
    164n16
"'Hombrecito,' The," 56–57
"Lady, A," 46, 51, 56
Obscene Bird of Night, The, 24, 25,
    29, 31, 32, 69, 82, 107, 108–37, 138,
    141, 144, 149, 150, 155n45, 161n18,
    165n5, 165n7, 166n16
"Paseo," 38–41, 42, 51–53, 54, 56,
    57–58
"Poisoned Pastries, The," 23, 156n1,
    158n23
Sacred Families, 25, 69, 138–47, 149
"Santelices," 43–45, 54, 57, 157n17
"Summertime," 34–35, 56, 148
This Sunday, 32, 35, 59, 71–88, 89,
    90, 104, 144, 149, 161n21, 162n28
"Tocayos," 55
Veraneo y otros cuentos, 23, 27

Donoso, José, Sr., 20
Dos Passos, John, 17; *Manhattan
    Transfer*, 28
Droguett, Carlos, 150; *Patas de Perro*,
Eloy, 17
Durand, Luis: *Frontera*, 16

Edwards, Jorge, 20, 150; *El peso de la
    noche*, 19
Ercilla, 24
Existentialism, 74, 79, 80, 94, 107,
    119–21, 136, 150, 157n19, 159n6,
    161n19, 161n24, 166–67n18; *see also*
    absurd, the; Sartre, Jean-Paul;
    Sartre's psychology
Expressionism, 159n26

Faulkner, William, 17, 20, 121, 150
Freud, Sigmund, 17, 38, 40, 45, 69,

73–74, 110, 119, 133, 156n3, 159n3, 160n13, 160–61n15, 161n17, 165n4, 165n5
Friedman, Norman, 164n16
Fromm, Erich, 156n11; *The Forgotten Language*, 156n9
Fuentes, Carlos, 25, 26, 30, 32, 108, 155n4; *Where the Air is Clear*, 28–29

Gallegos, Rómulo: *Doña Bárbara*, 16
García Márquez, Gabriel, 25; *One Hundred Years of Solitude*, 32
Generation of 1938, the, 16, 19
Generation of 1950, the, 18, 19, 20
Godoy, Juan: *Angurrientos*, 16, 17
Goic, Cedomil: *La novela chilena*, 15
Goya y Lucientes, Francisco de, 112–13; *Los caprichos*, 166n10
Grotesque, the, 162n28
Guido, Beatriz, 28
Güiraldes, Ricardo: *Don Segundo Sombra*, 16
Guzmán, Nicomedes, 17

Hades, 162–63n2
Hemingway, Ernest, 17, 55
Horney, Karen, 157n16; *The Neurotic Personality of Our Time*, 156n9
Hubner, Jorge, 19
Humberto Peñaloza (*The Obscene Bird of Night*), 108, 109, 110, 111, 112, 113, 115, 116, 117, 119, 120, 121, 123, 124, 125, 130, 131, 133, 136, 137, 141, 149, 150, 165–66n8

Icaza, Jorge: *The Villagers*, 16
Imbunche, 113, 131, 132, 166n12; *see also* Araucanian myth
Interior monologue, 162n27
Irony, 48–49, 64–65

James, Henry, 22, 57, 58, 65, 150
James, Henry, Sr., 169n39
Japonesita (*Hell Has No Limits*), 89, 94, 96, 97, 98, 100, 101, 102, 105, 106
Joyce, James, 17, 20, 121
Jung, Carl G., 40, 93, 111, 113, 119, 165n6, 166n14; *Man and His Symbols*, 161n18; *The Psychogenesis of Mental Disease*, 165n5; *The Portable Jung*, 166n9; *Psyche and Symbol*, 168–69n38

Kafka, Franz, 17; *The Metamorphosis*, 150

Lafourcade, Enrique, 18, 150; *Pena de muerte*, 20
Lainez, Mujica, 28
Laing, R.D.: *The Divided Self*, 160n7
Latorre, Mariano, 16
LaTour, Georges de, 106, 164n18, 165n19
Lazo, Jaime: *El cepo*, 20
Lillo Baldomero, 16

Machismo, 164n15
Mallea, Eduardo, 20
Manuela (*Hell Has Ho Limits*), 89, 90, 92, 93, 94, 96, 97–102, 103, 105, 106, 107, 149, 162–63n2, 163n5, 164n12
Marlowe, Christopher: *Doctor Faustus*, 162n1
Maya (*This Sunday*), 72, 75, 76, 77, 78, 79, 81, 82, 83 ,84, 85, 86, 87
Misiá Elisa (*Coronation*), 59, 60, 61, 64, 65, 66, 67, 68, 69, 70, 71, 87, 88, 160n7
Modernism, 123, 167n24
MSS, 23
Mudito (*The Obscene Bird of Night*), 110, 112, 113, 114, 115, 117, 118, 119, 122, 123, 124, 125, 127, 128, 129, 130, 131, 132, 133, 134, 135, 136, 137, 167n25, 168n36, 169n43
Muecke, D.C.: *Irony*, 158n21
Mundo Nuevo, 31, 32

Narcissus, 168n33
Naturalism, 15
Neruda, Pablo, 23, 27
Neumann, Erich: *The Origin and History of Consciousness*, 168n33

Ocampo, Victoria, 28
Onetti, Juan Carlos: *Brief Life, The Farewells*, 26

Padilla, Heberto, 32

Pancho Vega (*Hell Has No Limits*), 89,
93, 94–96, 97, 98, 100, 101, 102, 103,
104, 105, 106, 163n9, 164n11
Persona, the, 165n6, 168n33
Peta Ponce (*The Obscene Bird of Night*),
108, 110, 115, 116, 117, 118, 119, 124,
127, 128, 129, 136, 137, 169n43
Prado, Pedro, 17
Primera Plana, 155n39
Proust, Marcel, 22, 150, 160n11; *Remembrance of Things Past*, 73
Puig, Manuel, 33

Ravel, Maurice, 141, 142, 143, 144,
169–70n2
Realismo, 15, 153n3
Regionalism, 15, 26
Regionalist novels and novelists, 16
Rembrandt, 106, 164n18
Rivera, José Eustasio: *The Vortex*, 16
Roa Bastos, Augusto, 28
Rodríguez Monegal, Emir, 25, 26, 31,
33, 166n15; *El BOOM de la novela
latinoamericana*, 155n39
Rojas, Manuel, 17; *Hijo de ladrón*, 18
Rulfo, Juan: *Pedro Páramo*, 26

Sábato, Ernesto, 28; *The Outsider*, 26;
Sobre héroes y tumbas, 31, 155n42
Sadomasochism, 43, 45
Sainz, Gustavo, 33
Sarduy, Severo, 33
Sartre, Jean-Paul, 73, 74, 90, 91, 92,
107, 119, 120, 166–67n18

Sartre's psychology, 120–21, 160n14,
163n4, 163n8; *see also* Existentialism;
Sartre
Saturnus, 162–63n2
Schizophrenia, 110–13, 122, 133, 141–43
Serrano, María del Pilar, 21, 23
Shadow, the, 112, 157n13, 166n9
Siempre, 32, 155n39
Sisyphus, 91
Skármeta, Antonio, 33, 150
Stream-of-consciousness, 82–84, 121–24,
162n27
Surrealism, 46, 113–19, 135, 136, 150,
157n18, 164n12, 165n4, 166–67n18,
168n37
Symbiosis, 112, 165–66n8

Teiresias, 126, 167n25

Vallejo, César, 27
Vargas Llosa, Mario, 25; *The Time of the
Hero*, 30, 155n40; *Conversation in the
Cathedral*, 32; *The Green House*, 32
Vergara, Teresa, 21
Vidal, Hernán, *José Donoso: surrealismo
y rebelión de los instintos*, 164n12
Viñas, David, 28
Violeta (*This Sunday*), 72, 73, 74, 77, 78,
79, 81, 82, 83 ,84, 85, 86, 87

Woolf, Virginia, 17, 20, 121, 150

Yáñez, Alicia, 20, 22